Team Communication
Complete Self-Assessment Guide

The guidance in this Self-Assessment is based on Team Communication best practices and standards in business process architecture, design and quality management. The guidance is also based on the professional judgment of the individual collaborators listed in the Acknowledgments.

Notice of rights

You are licensed to use the Self-Assessment contents in your presentations and materials for internal use and customers without asking us - we are here to help.

Trademarks

Many of the designations used by manufacturers and sellers to distinguish their products are claimed as trademarks. Where those designations appear in this book, and the publisher was aware of a trademark claim, the designations appear as requested by the owner of the trademark. All other product names and services identified throughout this book are used in editorial fashion only and for the benefit of such companies with no intention of infringement of the trademark. No such use, or the use of any trade name, is intended to convey endorsement or other affiliation with this book.

Copyright © by The Art of Service
http://theartofservice.com
service@theartofservice.com

Table of Contents

About The Art of Service

The Art of Service, Business Process Architects since 2000, is dedicated to helping stakeholders achieve excellence.

Defining, designing, creating, and implementing a process to solve a stakeholders challenge or meet an objective is the most valuable role... In EVERY group, company, organization and department.

Unless you're talking a one-time, single-use project, there should be a process. Whether that process is managed and implemented by humans, AI, or a combination of the two, it needs to be designed by someone with a complex enough perspective to ask the right questions.

Someone capable of asking the right questions and step back and say, 'What are we really trying to accomplish here? And is there a different way to look at it?'

With The Art of Service's Standard Requirements Self-Assessments, we empower people who can do just that — whether their title is marketer, entrepreneur, manager, salesperson, consultant, Business Process Manager, executive assistant, IT Manager, CIO etc... —they are the people who rule the future. They are people who watch the process as it happens, and ask the right questions to make the process work better.

Contact us when you need any support with this Self-Assessment and any help with templates, blue-prints and examples of standard documents you might need:

http://theartofservice.com
service@theartofservice.com

Included Resources - how to access

Included with your purchase of the book is the Team

Communication Self-Assessment Spreadsheet Dashboard which contains all questions and Self-Assessment areas and auto-generates insights, graphs, and project RACI planning - all with examples to get you started right away.

How? Simply send an email to
access@theartofservice.com
with this books' title in the subject to get the Team Communication Self Assessment Tool right away.

You will receive the following contents with New and Updated specific criteria:

- The latest quick edition of the book in PDF

- The latest complete edition of the book in PDF, which criteria correspond to the criteria in...

- The Self-Assessment Excel Dashboard, and...

- Example pre-filled Self-Assessment Excel Dashboard to get familiar with results generation

- In-depth specific Checklists covering the topic

- Project management checklists and templates to assist with implementation

INCLUDES LIFETIME SELF ASSESSMENT UPDATES

Every self assessment comes with Lifetime Updates and Lifetime Free Updated Books. Lifetime Updates is an industry-first feature which allows you to receive verified self assessment updates, ensuring you always have the most accurate information at your fingertips.

Get it now- you will be glad you did - do it now, before you forget.

Send an email to **access@theartofservice.com** with this books' title in the subject to get the Team Communication Self Assessment Tool right away.

Purpose of this Self-Assessment

This Self-Assessment has been developed to improve understanding of the requirements and elements of Team Communication, based on best practices and standards in business process architecture, design and quality management.

It is designed to allow for a rapid Self-Assessment to determine how closely existing management practices and procedures correspond to the elements of the Self-Assessment.

The criteria of requirements and elements of Team Communication have been rephrased in the format of a Self-Assessment questionnaire, with a seven-criterion scoring system, as explained in this document.

In this format, even with limited background knowledge of Team Communication, a manager can quickly review existing operations to determine how they measure up to the standards. This in turn can serve as the starting point of a 'gap analysis' to identify management tools or system elements that might usefully be implemented in the organization to help improve overall performance.

How to use the Self-Assessment

On the following pages are a series of questions to identify to what extent your Team Communication initiative is complete in comparison to the requirements set in standards.

To facilitate answering the questions, there is a space in front of each question to enter a score on a scale of '1' to '5'.

1 Strongly Disagree

2 Disagree

3 Neutral

4 Agree

5 Strongly Agree

Read the question and rate it with the following in front of mind:

'In my belief, the answer to this question is clearly defined'.

There are two ways in which you can choose to interpret this statement;
1. how aware are you that the answer to the question is clearly defined
2. for more in-depth analysis you can choose to gather evidence and confirm the answer to the question. This obviously will take more time, most Self-Assessment users opt for the first way to interpret the question and dig deeper later on based on the outcome of the overall Self-Assessment.

A score of '1' would mean that the answer is not clear at all, where a '5' would mean the answer is crystal clear and defined. Leave emtpy when the question is not applicable or you don't want to answer it, you can skip it without affecting your score. Write your score in the space provided.

After you have responded to all the appropriate statements in each section, compute your average score for that section, using the formula provided, and round to the nearest tenth. Then transfer to the corresponding spoke in the Team Communication Scorecard on the second next page of the Self-Assessment.

Your completed Team Communication Scorecard will give you a clear presentation of which Team Communication areas need attention.

Team Communication Scorecard Example

Example of how the finalized Scorecard can look like:

Team Communication Scorecard

Your Scores:

BEGINNING OF THE SELF-ASSESSMENT:

CRITERION #1: RECOGNIZE

INTENT: Be aware of the need for change. Recognize that there is an unfavorable variation, problem or symptom.

In my belief, the answer to this question is clearly defined:

5 Strongly Agree

4 Agree

3 Neutral

2 Disagree

1 Strongly Disagree

1. Think about the people you identified for your team communication project and the project responsibilities you would assign to them, what kind of training do you think they would need to perform these responsibilities effectively?
<--- Score

2. Are you dealing with any of the same issues today as yesterday? What can you do about this?

<--- Score

3. Will a response program recognize when a crisis occurs and provide some level of response?
<--- Score

4. Which information does the team communication business case need to include?
<--- Score

5. What is the problem or issue?
<--- Score

6. When a team communication manager recognizes a problem, what options are available?
<--- Score

7. Do you have/need 24-hour access to key personnel?
<--- Score

8. Will it solve real problems?
<--- Score

9. Is it clear when you think of the day ahead of you what activities and tasks you need to complete?
<--- Score

10. What are the stakeholder objectives to be achieved with team communication?
<--- Score

11. What else needs to be measured?
<--- Score

12. What does team communication success mean to the stakeholders?

<--- Score

13. Which issues are too important to ignore?
<--- Score

14. Who needs to know about team communication?
<--- Score

15. What tools and technologies are needed for a custom team communication project?
<--- Score

16. How can auditing be a preventative security measure?
<--- Score

17. How do you identify subcontractor relationships?
<--- Score

18. What problems are you facing and how do you consider team communication will circumvent those obstacles?
<--- Score

19. Are losses recognized in a timely manner?
<--- Score

20. What information do users need?
<--- Score

21. What are the expected benefits of team communication to the stakeholder?
<--- Score

22. Is the quality assurance team identified?
<--- Score

23. Who are your key stakeholders who need to sign off?
<--- Score

24. Does team communication create potential expectations in other areas that need to be recognized and considered?
<--- Score

25. Are there any specific expectations or concerns about the team communication team, team communication itself?
<--- Score

26. What is the recognized need?
<--- Score

27. Consider your own team communication project, what types of organizational problems do you think might be causing or affecting your problem, based on the work done so far?
<--- Score

28. What extra resources will you need?
<--- Score

29. Are employees recognized or rewarded for performance that demonstrates the highest levels of integrity?
<--- Score

30. How do you assess your team communication workforce capability and capacity needs, including skills, competencies, and staffing levels?
<--- Score

31. What training and capacity building actions are needed to implement proposed reforms?
<--- Score

32. What vendors make products that address the team communication needs?
<--- Score

33. Did you miss any major team communication issues?
<--- Score

34. How many trainings, in total, are needed?
<--- Score

35. Are there any revenue recognition issues?
<--- Score

36. To what extent would your organization benefit from being recognized as a award recipient?
<--- Score

37. Whom do you really need or want to serve?
<--- Score

38. How much are sponsors, customers, partners, stakeholders involved in team communication? In other words, what are the risks, if team communication does not deliver successfully?
<--- Score

39. Why the need?
<--- Score

40. How do you take a forward-looking perspective in

identifying team communication research related to
market response and models?
<--- Score

41. Have you identified your team communication key
performance indicators?
<--- Score

42. What is the extent or complexity of the team
communication problem?
<--- Score

43. What is the smallest subset of the problem you
can usefully solve?
<--- Score

44. How do you recognize an objection?
<--- Score

45. How are training requirements identified?
<--- Score

46. How are the team communication's objectives
aligned to the group's overall stakeholder strategy?
<--- Score

47. What needs to be done?
<--- Score

48. What resources or support might you need?
<--- Score

49. What prevents you from making the changes
you know will make you a more effective team
communication leader?
<--- Score

50. For your team communication project, identify and describe the business environment, is there more than one layer to the business environment?
<--- Score

51. How does it fit into your organizational needs and tasks?
<--- Score

52. Are problem definition and motivation clearly presented?
<--- Score

53. Do you need to avoid or amend any team communication activities?
<--- Score

54. What are the team communication resources needed?
<--- Score

55. What should be considered when identifying available resources, constraints, and deadlines?
<--- Score

56. Who else hopes to benefit from it?
<--- Score

57. What team communication capabilities do you need?
<--- Score

58. Where do you need to exercise leadership?
<--- Score

59. What team communication problem should be solved?
<--- Score

60. What creative shifts do you need to take?
<--- Score

61. As a sponsor, customer or management, how important is it to meet goals, objectives?
<--- Score

62. What is the team communication problem definition? What do you need to resolve?
<--- Score

63. What team communication events should you attend?
<--- Score

64. What do you need to start doing?
<--- Score

65. Will team communication deliverables need to be tested and, if so, by whom?
<--- Score

66. What activities does the governance board need to consider?
<--- Score

67. Where is training needed?
<--- Score

68. Are your goals realistic? Do you need to redefine your problem? Perhaps the problem has changed or maybe you have reached your goal and need to set a

new one?
<--- Score

69. Is the need for organizational change recognized?
<--- Score

70. How do you identify the kinds of information that you will need?
<--- Score

71. What are the minority interests and what amount of minority interests can be recognized?
<--- Score

72. What situation(s) led to this team communication Self Assessment?
<--- Score

73. To what extent does each concerned units management team recognize team communication as an effective investment?
<--- Score

74. How are you going to measure success?
<--- Score

75. Are controls defined to recognize and contain problems?
<--- Score

76. How do you recognize an team communication objection?
<--- Score

77. Will new equipment/products be required to facilitate team communication delivery, for example is

new software needed?
<--- Score

78. Are employees recognized for desired behaviors?
<--- Score

79. Who needs budgets?
<--- Score

80. What would happen if team communication weren't done?
<--- Score

81. Are there team communication problems defined?
<--- Score

82. Does your organization need more team communication education?
<--- Score

83. What do employees need in the short term?
<--- Score

84. Who needs what information?
<--- Score

85. Why is this needed?
<--- Score

86. Does the problem have ethical dimensions?
<--- Score

87. Who defines the rules in relation to any given issue?
<--- Score

88. Do you need different information or graphics?
<--- Score

89. Are there recognized team communication problems?
<--- Score

90. Is it needed?
<--- Score

91. Are there regulatory / compliance issues?
<--- Score

92. Who should resolve the team communication issues?
<--- Score

Add up total points for this section:
_ _ _ _ _ = Total points for this section

Divided by: _ _ _ _ _ _ (number of statements answered) = _ _ _ _ _ _
Average score for this section

Transfer your score to the team communication Index at the beginning of the Self-Assessment.

CRITERION #2: DEFINE:

INTENT: Formulate the stakeholder problem. Define the problem, needs and objectives.

In my belief, the answer to this question is clearly defined:

5 Strongly Agree

4 Agree

3 Neutral

2 Disagree

1 Strongly Disagree

1. What knowledge or experience is required?
<--- Score

2. What is out of scope?
<--- Score

3. How and when will the baselines be defined?
<--- Score

4. What are (control) requirements for team communication Information?
<--- Score

5. Are there different segments of customers?
<--- Score

6. If substitutes have been appointed, have they been briefed on the team communication goals and received regular communications as to the progress to date?
<--- Score

7. What is in scope?
<--- Score

8. What are the team communication tasks and definitions?
<--- Score

9. Is there a completed, verified, and validated high-level 'as is' (not 'should be' or 'could be') stakeholder process map?
<--- Score

10. What is the scope?
<--- Score

11. Have all basic functions of team communication been defined?
<--- Score

12. How do you catch team communication definition inconsistencies?
<--- Score

13. What team communication services do you require?
<--- Score

14. What are the dynamics of the communication plan?
<--- Score

15. Has a team communication requirement not been met?
<--- Score

16. What intelligence can you gather?
<--- Score

17. How do you manage scope?
<--- Score

18. Is the team equipped with available and reliable resources?
<--- Score

19. Is the team communication scope manageable?
<--- Score

20. In what way can you redefine the criteria of choice clients have in your category in your favor?
<--- Score

21. How are consistent team communication definitions important?
<--- Score

22. What happens if team communication's scope changes?
<--- Score

23. Who is gathering information?
<--- Score

24. Scope of sensitive information?
<--- Score

25. What is the definition of success?
<--- Score

26. What are the core elements of the team communication business case?
<--- Score

27. Have the customer needs been translated into specific, measurable requirements? How?
<--- Score

28. Has a high-level 'as is' process map been completed, verified and validated?
<--- Score

29. How will variation in the actual durations of each activity be dealt with to ensure that the expected team communication results are met?
<--- Score

30. What customer feedback methods were used to solicit their input?
<--- Score

31. What is the scope of the team communication effort?
<--- Score

32. Has the direction changed at all during the course

of team communication? If so, when did it change and why?
<--- Score

33. What specifically is the problem? Where does it occur? When does it occur? What is its extent?
<--- Score

34. Is the work to date meeting requirements?
<--- Score

35. Is there a team communication management charter, including stakeholder case, problem and goal statements, scope, milestones, roles and responsibilities, communication plan?
<--- Score

36. What is the scope of team communication?
<--- Score

37. Will team members perform team communication work when assigned and in a timely fashion?
<--- Score

38. How is the team tracking and documenting its work?
<--- Score

39. Who approved the team communication scope?
<--- Score

40. Is there a critical path to deliver team communication results?
<--- Score

41. What are the team communication use cases?

<--- Score

42. How do you gather the stories?
<--- Score

43. How do you gather requirements?
<--- Score

44. What baselines are required to be defined and managed?
<--- Score

45. Are required metrics defined, what are they?
<--- Score

46. Has a project plan, Gantt chart, or similar been developed/completed?
<--- Score

47. How do you manage changes in team communication requirements?
<--- Score

48. Is team communication required?
<--- Score

49. What scope to assess?
<--- Score

50. What constraints exist that might impact the team?
<--- Score

51. How have you defined all team communication requirements first?
<--- Score

52. Is there regularly 100% attendance at the team meetings? If not, have appointed substitutes attended to preserve cross-functionality and full representation?
<--- Score

53. How can the value of team communication be defined?
<--- Score

54. What is the worst case scenario?
<--- Score

55. Are there any constraints known that bear on the ability to perform team communication work? How is the team addressing them?
<--- Score

56. What are the requirements for audit information?
<--- Score

57. Has everyone on the team, including the team leaders, been properly trained?
<--- Score

58. How do you build the right business case?
<--- Score

59. Is it clearly defined in and to your organization what you do?
<--- Score

60. Is special team communication user knowledge required?
<--- Score

61. When is/was the team communication start date?
<--- Score

62. When are meeting minutes sent out? Who is on the distribution list?
<--- Score

63. Is the scope of team communication defined?
<--- Score

64. How does the team communication manager ensure against scope creep?
<--- Score

65. How was the 'as is' process map developed, reviewed, verified and validated?
<--- Score

66. Has the team communication work been fairly and/or equitably divided and delegated among team members who are qualified and capable to perform the work? Has everyone contributed?
<--- Score

67. Are the team communication requirements testable?
<--- Score

68. How would you define team communication leadership?
<--- Score

69. Who is gathering team communication information?
<--- Score

70. Where can you gather more information?
<--- Score

71. How did the team communication manager receive input to the development of a team communication improvement plan and the estimated completion dates/times of each activity?
<--- Score

72. Why are you doing team communication and what is the scope?
<--- Score

73. Has the improvement team collected the 'voice of the customer' (obtained feedback – qualitative and quantitative)?
<--- Score

74. Has/have the customer(s) been identified?
<--- Score

75. What is the scope of the team communication work?
<--- Score

76. Who defines (or who defined) the rules and roles?
<--- Score

77. When is the estimated completion date?
<--- Score

78. Are task requirements clearly defined?
<--- Score

79. What are the rough order estimates on cost

savings/opportunities that team communication brings?
<--- Score

80. What are the record-keeping requirements of team communication activities?
<--- Score

81. How do you manage unclear team communication requirements?
<--- Score

82. Is scope creep really all bad news?
<--- Score

83. Is the current 'as is' process being followed? If not, what are the discrepancies?
<--- Score

84. What is the definition of team communication excellence?
<--- Score

85. Are the team communication requirements complete?
<--- Score

86. What is in the scope and what is not in scope?
<--- Score

87. How will the team communication team and the group measure complete success of team communication?
<--- Score

88. Are roles and responsibilities formally defined?

<--- Score

89. How do you think the partners involved in team communication would have defined success?
<--- Score

90. Will a team communication production readiness review be required?
<--- Score

91. What are the compelling stakeholder reasons for embarking on team communication?
<--- Score

92. Have all of the relationships been defined properly?
<--- Score

93. Have specific policy objectives been defined?
<--- Score

94. Is the team formed and are team leaders (Coaches and Management Leads) assigned?
<--- Score

95. Who are the team communication improvement team members, including Management Leads and Coaches?
<--- Score

96. What is the context?
<--- Score

97. What sources do you use to gather information for a team communication study?
<--- Score

98. Is team communication currently on schedule according to the plan?
<--- Score

99. What critical content must be communicated – who, what, when, where, and how?
<--- Score

100. How often are the team meetings?
<--- Score

101. Are improvement team members fully trained on team communication?
<--- Score

102. What scope do you want your strategy to cover?
<--- Score

103. Are different versions of process maps needed to account for the different types of inputs?
<--- Score

104. What gets examined?
<--- Score

105. How would you define the culture at your organization, how susceptible is it to team communication changes?
<--- Score

106. Will team members regularly document their team communication work?
<--- Score

107. How do you gather team communication

requirements?
<--- Score

108. Are accountability and ownership for team communication clearly defined?
<--- Score

109. Is there any additional team communication definition of success?
<--- Score

110. Is the team sponsored by a champion or stakeholder leader?
<--- Score

111. What system do you use for gathering team communication information?
<--- Score

112. What sort of initial information to gather?
<--- Score

113. What is out-of-scope initially?
<--- Score

114. Do you have a team communication success story or case study ready to tell and share?
<--- Score

115. Does the team have regular meetings?
<--- Score

116. Has anyone else (internal or external to the group) attempted to solve this problem or a similar one before? If so, what knowledge can be leveraged from these previous efforts?

<--- Score

117. Are all requirements met?
<--- Score

118. What would be the goal or target for a team communication's improvement team?
<--- Score

119. Is team communication linked to key stakeholder goals and objectives?
<--- Score

120. Is full participation by members in regularly held team meetings guaranteed?
<--- Score

121. What key stakeholder process output measure(s) does team communication leverage and how?
<--- Score

122. Is there a completed SIPOC representation, describing the Suppliers, Inputs, Process, Outputs, and Customers?
<--- Score

123. Do the problem and goal statements meet the SMART criteria (specific, measurable, attainable, relevant, and time-bound)?
<--- Score

124. What are the boundaries of the scope? What is in bounds and what is not? What is the start point? What is the stop point?
<--- Score

125. How do you keep key subject matter experts in the loop?
<--- Score

126. Are approval levels defined for contracts and supplements to contracts?
<--- Score

127. The political context: who holds power?
<--- Score

128. Are customer(s) identified and segmented according to their different needs and requirements?
<--- Score

129. Is the team adequately staffed with the desired cross-functionality? If not, what additional resources are available to the team?
<--- Score

130. What are the Roles and Responsibilities for each team member and its leadership? Where is this documented?
<--- Score

131. Is the improvement team aware of the different versions of a process: what they think it is vs. what it actually is vs. what it should be vs. what it could be?
<--- Score

132. Has a team charter been developed and communicated?
<--- Score

133. What defines best in class?
<--- Score

134. Are resources adequate for the scope?
<--- Score

135. What is a worst-case scenario for losses?
<--- Score

136. Is data collected and displayed to better understand customer(s) critical needs and requirements.
<--- Score

137. Is the team communication scope complete and appropriately sized?
<--- Score

138. What are the tasks and definitions?
<--- Score

Add up total points for this section:
_____ = Total points for this section

Divided by: _____ (number of statements answered) = _____
Average score for this section

Transfer your score to the team communication Index at the beginning of the Self-Assessment.

CRITERION #3: MEASURE:

INTENT: Gather the correct data.
Measure the current performance and
evolution of the situation.

In my belief, the answer to this
question is clearly defined:

5 Strongly Agree

4 Agree

3 Neutral

2 Disagree

1 Strongly Disagree

1. How are measurements made?
<--- Score

2. How frequently do you track team communication
measures?
<--- Score

3. Why do the measurements/indicators matter?
<--- Score

4. What evidence is there and what is measured?
<--- Score

5. What are the types and number of measures to use?
<--- Score

6. What potential environmental factors impact the team communication effort?
<--- Score

7. How are costs allocated?
<--- Score

8. Will team communication have an impact on current business continuity, disaster recovery processes and/or infrastructure?
<--- Score

9. Did you tackle the cause or the symptom?
<--- Score

10. What are your key team communication organizational performance measures, including key short and longer-term financial measures?
<--- Score

11. What are you verifying?
<--- Score

12. What users will be impacted?
<--- Score

13. What causes extra work or rework?
<--- Score

14. Are the measurements objective?
<--- Score

15. What do you measure and why?
<--- Score

16. Do you have any cost team communication limitation requirements?
<--- Score

17. Who should receive measurement reports?
<--- Score

18. What are the operational costs after team communication deployment?
<--- Score

19. Are the units of measure consistent?
<--- Score

20. What is the cost of rework?
<--- Score

21. Are team communication vulnerabilities categorized and prioritized?
<--- Score

22. What tests verify requirements?
<--- Score

23. Do the benefits outweigh the costs?
<--- Score

24. How do you verify performance?
<--- Score

25. What does a Test Case verify?
<--- Score

26. What harm might be caused?
<--- Score

27. What does losing customers cost your organization?
<--- Score

28. Do you aggressively reward and promote the people who have the biggest impact on creating excellent team communication services/products?
<--- Score

29. At what cost?
<--- Score

30. How much does it cost?
<--- Score

31. How will measures be used to manage and adapt?
<--- Score

32. How do you measure lifecycle phases?
<--- Score

33. What could cause you to change course?
<--- Score

34. When are costs are incurred?
<--- Score

35. How do you verify the team communication requirements quality?
<--- Score

36. When should you bother with diagrams?
<--- Score

37. How long to keep data and how to manage retention costs?
<--- Score

38. Who is involved in verifying compliance?
<--- Score

39. When a disaster occurs, who gets priority?
<--- Score

40. Why do you expend time and effort to implement measurement, for whom?
<--- Score

41. What is your team communication quality cost segregation study?
<--- Score

42. What do people want to verify?
<--- Score

43. What measurements are being captured?
<--- Score

44. What measurements are possible, practicable and meaningful?
<--- Score

45. How do you aggregate measures across priorities?
<--- Score

46. What are the strategic priorities for this year?

<--- Score

47. Does management have the right priorities among projects?
<--- Score

48. What is the cause of any team communication gaps?
<--- Score

49. Who pays the cost?
<--- Score

50. How is performance measured?
<--- Score

51. Does the team communication task fit the client's priorities?
<--- Score

52. Where is it measured?
<--- Score

53. How do you verify and develop ideas and innovations?
<--- Score

54. How do you control the overall costs of your work processes?
<--- Score

55. Do you verify that corrective actions were taken?
<--- Score

56. Are there competing team communication priorities?

<--- Score

57. How to cause the change?
<--- Score

58. What is measured? Why?
<--- Score

59. Is the solution cost-effective?
<--- Score

60. What are the costs?
<--- Score

61. What is your decision requirements diagram?
<--- Score

62. How sensitive must the team communication strategy be to cost?
<--- Score

63. Have design-to-cost goals been established?
<--- Score

64. Are you aware of what could cause a problem?
<--- Score

65. How will you measure success?
<--- Score

66. How can a team communication test verify your ideas or assumptions?
<--- Score

67. What causes mismanagement?
<--- Score

68. What causes innovation to fail or succeed in your organization?
<--- Score

69. Is it possible to estimate the impact of unanticipated complexity such as wrong or failed assumptions, feedback, etcetera on proposed reforms?
<--- Score

70. What are the costs of reform?
<--- Score

71. What are the team communication key cost drivers?
<--- Score

72. How will you measure your team communication effectiveness?
<--- Score

73. How do you verify if team communication is built right?
<--- Score

74. How do you measure success?
<--- Score

75. What methods are feasible and acceptable to estimate the impact of reforms?
<--- Score

76. What are the estimated costs of proposed changes?
<--- Score

77. What details are required of the team communication cost structure?
<--- Score

78. How is the value delivered by team communication being measured?
<--- Score

79. What drives O&M cost?
<--- Score

80. Where can you go to verify the info?
<--- Score

81. What are the team communication investment costs?
<--- Score

82. Do you have a flow diagram of what happens?
<--- Score

83. How can you reduce costs?
<--- Score

84. What is an unallowable cost?
<--- Score

85. Was a business case (cost/benefit) developed?
<--- Score

86. What are your operating costs?
<--- Score

87. Is there an opportunity to verify requirements?
<--- Score

88. How can you measure team communication in a systematic way?
<--- Score

89. How do you measure efficient delivery of team communication services?
<--- Score

90. What does your operating model cost?
<--- Score

91. What disadvantage does this cause for the user?
<--- Score

92. Have you made assumptions about the shape of the future, particularly its impact on your customers and competitors?
<--- Score

93. Are actual costs in line with budgeted costs?
<--- Score

94. What are the costs and benefits?
<--- Score

95. What would it cost to replace your technology?
<--- Score

96. What are your customers expectations and measures?
<--- Score

97. How can you measure the performance?
<--- Score

98. How do you quantify and qualify impacts?
<--- Score

99. How can you manage cost down?
<--- Score

100. Have you included everything in your team communication cost models?
<--- Score

101. Does a team communication quantification method exist?
<--- Score

102. What is the total cost related to deploying team communication, including any consulting or professional services?
<--- Score

103. Where is the cost?
<--- Score

104. Are indirect costs charged to the team communication program?
<--- Score

105. Are there any easy-to-implement alternatives to team communication? Sometimes other solutions are available that do not require the cost implications of a full-blown project?
<--- Score

106. Are supply costs steady or fluctuating?
<--- Score

107. How can you reduce the costs of obtaining

inputs?
<--- Score

108. How will success or failure be measured?
<--- Score

109. Are you able to realize any cost savings?
<--- Score

110. Which team communication impacts are significant?
<--- Score

111. How do you prevent mis-estimating cost?
<--- Score

112. Which costs should be taken into account?
<--- Score

113. How do you measure variability?
<--- Score

114. How do you verify and validate the team communication data?
<--- Score

115. What is the total fixed cost?
<--- Score

116. Do you have an issue in getting priority?
<--- Score

117. How will your organization measure success?
<--- Score

118. What are the uncertainties surrounding estimates

of impact?

<--- Score

119. What causes investor action?

<--- Score

120. Among the team communication product and service cost to be estimated, which is considered hardest to estimate?

<--- Score

121. How do you verify your resources?

<--- Score

122. What are the costs of delaying team communication action?

<--- Score

123. How do you verify the authenticity of the data and information used?

<--- Score

124. What is the root cause(s) of the problem?

<--- Score

125. Do you effectively measure and reward individual and team performance?

<--- Score

126. Which measures and indicators matter?

<--- Score

127. What is the team communication business impact?

<--- Score

128. How will effects be measured?
<--- Score

129. How will costs be allocated?
<--- Score

130. What are the current costs of the team communication process?
<--- Score

131. How is progress measured?
<--- Score

132. What are hidden team communication quality costs?
<--- Score

133. What are your primary costs, revenues, assets?
<--- Score

134. What could cause delays in the schedule?
<--- Score

135. What can be used to verify compliance?
<--- Score

136. Are the team communication benefits worth its costs?
<--- Score

Add up total points for this section:
_ _ _ _ _ = Total points for this section

Divided by: _ _ _ _ _ _ (number of statements answered) = _ _ _ _ _ _
Average score for this section

Transfer your score to the team
communication Index at the beginning
of the Self-Assessment.

CRITERION #4: ANALYZE:

INTENT: Analyze causes, assumptions
and hypotheses.

In my belief, the answer to this
question is clearly defined:

5 Strongly Agree

4 Agree

3 Neutral

2 Disagree

1 Strongly Disagree

1. What output to create?
<--- Score

2. What team communication metrics are outputs of
the process?
<--- Score

3. How will corresponding data be collected?
<--- Score

4. What systems/processes must you excel at?
<--- Score

5. Do your leaders quickly bounce back from setbacks?
<--- Score

6. What are your outputs?
<--- Score

7. What team communication data will be collected?
<--- Score

8. Can you add value to the current team communication decision-making process (largely qualitative) by incorporating uncertainty modeling (more quantitative)?
<--- Score

9. What are your best practices for minimizing team communication project risk, while demonstrating incremental value and quick wins throughout the team communication project lifecycle?
<--- Score

10. How is the team communication Value Stream Mapping managed?
<--- Score

11. What training and qualifications will you need?
<--- Score

12. How do you implement and manage your work processes to ensure that they meet design requirements?
<--- Score

13. What are the team communication design outputs?
<--- Score

14. Do several people in different organizational units assist with the team communication process?
<--- Score

15. How do you define collaboration and team output?
<--- Score

16. Is there any way to speed up the process?
<--- Score

17. How many input/output points does it require?
<--- Score

18. Have the problem and goal statements been updated to reflect the additional knowledge gained from the analyze phase?
<--- Score

19. How much data can be collected in the given timeframe?
<--- Score

20. What qualifications are necessary?
<--- Score

21. What is your organizations process which leads to recognition of value generation?
<--- Score

22. Was a cause-and-effect diagram used to explore

the different types of causes (or sources of variation)?
<--- Score

23. What are the revised rough estimates of the financial savings/opportunity for team communication improvements?
<--- Score

24. What team communication data should be managed?
<--- Score

25. What are the necessary qualifications?
<--- Score

26. What tools were used to narrow the list of possible causes?
<--- Score

27. A compounding model resolution with available relevant data can often provide insight towards a solution methodology; which team communication models, tools and techniques are necessary?
<--- Score

28. Who is involved in the management review process?
<--- Score

29. How do mission and objectives affect the team communication processes of your organization?
<--- Score

30. What controls do you have in place to protect data?
<--- Score

31. How is the way you as the leader think and process information affecting your organizational culture?
<--- Score

32. Were there any improvement opportunities identified from the process analysis?
<--- Score

33. How do you measure the operational performance of your key work systems and processes, including productivity, cycle time, and other appropriate measures of process effectiveness, efficiency, and innovation?
<--- Score

34. What is the oversight process?
<--- Score

35. What data do you need to collect?
<--- Score

36. Did any value-added analysis or 'lean thinking' take place to identify some of the gaps shown on the 'as is' process map?
<--- Score

37. Think about the functions involved in your team communication project, what processes flow from these functions?
<--- Score

38. Are gaps between current performance and the goal performance identified?
<--- Score

39. Where is the data coming from to measure compliance?
<--- Score

40. How can risk management be tied procedurally to process elements?
<--- Score

41. What qualifications are needed?
<--- Score

42. What qualifications do team communication leaders need?
<--- Score

43. What resources go in to get the desired output?
<--- Score

44. What did the team gain from developing a sub-process map?
<--- Score

45. How is team communication data gathered?
<--- Score

46. How do you use team communication data and information to support organizational decision making and innovation?
<--- Score

47. How do you ensure that the team communication opportunity is realistic?
<--- Score

48. Who qualifies to gain access to data?
<--- Score

49. Is data and process analysis, root cause analysis and quantifying the gap/opportunity in place?
<--- Score

50. Which team communication data should be retained?
<--- Score

51. What is the output?
<--- Score

52. What kind of crime could a potential new hire have committed that would not only not disqualify him/her from being hired by your organization, but would actually indicate that he/she might be a particularly good fit?
<--- Score

53. What conclusions were drawn from the team's data collection and analysis? How did the team reach these conclusions?
<--- Score

54. Were Pareto charts (or similar) used to portray the 'heavy hitters' (or key sources of variation)?
<--- Score

55. What are your current levels and trends in key team communication measures or indicators of product and process performance that are important to and directly serve your customers?
<--- Score

56. Is pre-qualification of suppliers carried out?
<--- Score

57. What, related to, team communication processes does your organization outsource?
<--- Score

58. How has the team communication data been gathered?
<--- Score

59. What are the disruptive team communication technologies that enable your organization to radically change your business processes?
<--- Score

60. Is there an established change management process?
<--- Score

61. Do you understand your management processes today?
<--- Score

62. What are your current levels and trends in key measures or indicators of team communication product and process performance that are important to and directly serve your customers? How do these results compare with the performance of your competitors and other organizations with similar offerings?
<--- Score

63. Are all team members qualified for all tasks?
<--- Score

64. How do you promote understanding that opportunity for improvement is not criticism of the

status quo, or the people who created the status quo?
<--- Score

65. Where can you get qualified talent today?
<--- Score

66. What are the processes for audit reporting and management?
<--- Score

67. Who owns what data?
<--- Score

68. What do you need to qualify?
<--- Score

69. Should you invest in industry-recognized qualifications?
<--- Score

70. Are all staff in core team communication subjects Highly Qualified?
<--- Score

71. What are the team communication business drivers?
<--- Score

72. Do quality systems drive continuous improvement?
<--- Score

73. What information qualified as important?
<--- Score

74. Has an output goal been set?

<--- Score

75. What quality tools were used to get through the analyze phase?
<--- Score

76. Do you, as a leader, bounce back quickly from setbacks?
<--- Score

77. How was the detailed process map generated, verified, and validated?
<--- Score

78. Who gets your output?
<--- Score

79. What are the best opportunities for value improvement?
<--- Score

80. Are you missing team communication opportunities?
<--- Score

81. What are the personnel training and qualifications required?
<--- Score

82. What other jobs or tasks affect the performance of the steps in the team communication process?
<--- Score

83. What internal processes need improvement?
<--- Score

84. What is the cost of poor quality as supported by the team's analysis?
<--- Score

85. Are team communication changes recognized early enough to be approved through the regular process?
<--- Score

86. What is your organizations system for selecting qualified vendors?
<--- Score

87. When should a process be art not science?
<--- Score

88. What process improvements will be needed?
<--- Score

89. What qualifies as competition?
<--- Score

90. How do you identify specific team communication investment opportunities and emerging trends?
<--- Score

91. Were any designed experiments used to generate additional insight into the data analysis?
<--- Score

92. What tools were used to generate the list of possible causes?
<--- Score

93. What is the team communication Driver?
<--- Score

94. Is the performance gap determined?
<--- Score

95. How will the change process be managed?
<--- Score

96. How difficult is it to qualify what team communication ROI is?
<--- Score

97. Did any additional data need to be collected?
<--- Score

98. What are your team communication processes?
<--- Score

99. What does the data say about the performance of the stakeholder process?
<--- Score

100. What methods do you use to gather team communication data?
<--- Score

101. Are your outputs consistent?
<--- Score

102. Is the suppliers process defined and controlled?
< Score

103. Is the required team communication data gathered?
<--- Score

104. How is the data gathered?

<--- Score

105. Do you have the authority to produce the output?
<--- Score

106. Who is involved with workflow mapping?
<--- Score

107. Record-keeping requirements flow from the records needed as inputs, outputs, controls and for transformation of a team communication process, are the records needed as inputs to the team communication process available?
<--- Score

108. Is the gap/opportunity displayed and communicated in financial terms?
<--- Score

109. Who will facilitate the team and process?
<--- Score

110. Was a detailed process map created to amplify critical steps of the 'as is' stakeholder process?
<--- Score

111. How do your work systems and key work processes relate to and capitalize on your core competencies?
<--- Score

112. Who will gather what data?
<--- Score

113. What team communication data should be

collected?
<--- Score

114. What are your key performance measures or indicators and in-process measures for the control and improvement of your team communication processes?
<--- Score

115. What were the financial benefits resulting from any 'ground fruit or low-hanging fruit' (quick fixes)?
<--- Score

116. Do your employees have the opportunity to do what they do best everyday?
<--- Score

117. How will the data be checked for quality?
<--- Score

118. What types of data do your team communication indicators require?
<--- Score

119. How is data used for program management and improvement?
<--- Score

120. Is the team communication process severely broken such that a re-design is necessary?
<--- Score

121. What qualifications and skills do you need?
<--- Score

122. What is the complexity of the output produced?

<--- Score

123. Is there a strict change management process?
<--- Score

124. What data is gathered?
<--- Score

125. What will drive team communication change?
<--- Score

126. Is the final output clearly identified?
<--- Score

127. What team communication data do you gather or use now?
<--- Score

128. How are outputs preserved and protected?
<--- Score

129. Have any additional benefits been identified that will result from closing all or most of the gaps?
<--- Score

130. Identify an operational issue in your organization, for example, could a particular task be done more quickly or more efficiently by team communication?
<--- Score

131. How does the organization define, manage, and improve its team communication processes?
<--- Score

132. Has data output been validated?
<--- Score

133. An organizationally feasible system request is one that considers the mission, goals and objectives of the organization, key questions are: is the team communication solution request practical and will it solve a problem or take advantage of an opportunity to achieve company goals?
<--- Score

134. How often will data be collected for measures?
<--- Score

135. What were the crucial 'moments of truth' on the process map?
<--- Score

136. Have you defined which data is gathered how?
<--- Score

137. What process should you select for improvement?
<--- Score

138. How will the team communication data be captured?
<--- Score

Add up total points for this section:
_ _ _ _ _ = Total points for this section

Divided by: _ _ _ _ _ _ (number of statements answered) = _ _ _ _ _ _
Average score for this section

Transfer your score to the team communication Index at the beginning

of the Self-Assessment.

CRITERION #5: IMPROVE:

INTENT: Develop a practical solution. Innovate, establish and test the solution and to measure the results.

In my belief, the answer to this question is clearly defined:

5 Strongly Agree

4 Agree

3 Neutral

2 Disagree

1 Strongly Disagree

1. How do you manage and improve your team communication work systems to deliver customer value and achieve organizational success and sustainability?
<--- Score

2. What tools were used to evaluate the potential solutions?
<--- Score

3. What tools were most useful during the improve phase?
<--- Score

4. Who are the people involved in developing and implementing team communication?
<--- Score

5. Have you identified breakpoints and/or risk tolerances that will trigger broad consideration of a potential need for intervention or modification of strategy?
<--- Score

6. What lessons, if any, from a pilot were incorporated into the design of the full-scale solution?
<--- Score

7. How can you improve performance?
<--- Score

8. Are the risks fully understood, reasonable and manageable?
<--- Score

9. If you could go back in time five years, what decision would you make differently? What is your best guess as to what decision you're making today you might regret five years from now?
<--- Score

10. How do you link measurement and risk?
<--- Score

11. Do those selected for the team communication

team have a good general understanding of what team communication is all about?
<--- Score

12. Do vendor agreements bring new compliance risk ?
<--- Score

13. Is there a small-scale pilot for proposed improvement(s)? What conclusions were drawn from the outcomes of a pilot?
<--- Score

14. Is the team communication documentation thorough?
<--- Score

15. For estimation problems, how do you develop an estimation statement?
<--- Score

16. Who are the team communication decision makers?
<--- Score

17. Do you have the optimal project management team structure?
<--- Score

18. How does the team improve its work?
<--- Score

19. When you map the key players in your own work and the types/domains of relationships with them, which relationships do you find easy and which challenging, and why?

<--- Score

20. What current systems have to be understood and/ or changed?
<--- Score

21. What area needs the greatest improvement?
<--- Score

22. How will you know that a change is an improvement?
<--- Score

23. Will the controls trigger any other risks?
<--- Score

24. Who controls key decisions that will be made?
<--- Score

25. What are the concrete team communication results?
<--- Score

26. At what point will vulnerability assessments be performed once team communication is put into production (e.g., ongoing Risk Management after implementation)?
<--- Score

27. What actually has to improve and by how much?
<--- Score

28. What is the team communication's sustainability risk?
<--- Score

29. How do you improve productivity?
<--- Score

30. team communication risk decisions: whose call Is It?
<--- Score

31. How can skill-level changes improve team communication?
<--- Score

32. Explorations of the frontiers of team communication will help you build influence, improve team communication, optimize decision making, and sustain change, what is your approach?
<--- Score

33. How do you measure progress and evaluate training effectiveness?
<--- Score

34. What were the criteria for evaluating a team communication pilot?
<--- Score

35. Have you achieved team communication improvements?
<--- Score

36. What are the affordable team communication risks?
<--- Score

37. What risks do you need to manage?
<--- Score

38. What attendant changes will need to be made to ensure that the solution is successful?
<--- Score

39. What is team communication risk?
<--- Score

40. How do you improve team communication service perception, and satisfaction?
<--- Score

41. In the past few months, what is the smallest change you have made that has had the biggest positive result? What was it about that small change that produced the large return?
<--- Score

42. How will you know when its improved?
<--- Score

43. Does the goal represent a desired result that can be measured?
<--- Score

44. How do the team communication results compare with the performance of your competitors and other organizations with similar offerings?
<--- Score

45. How do you keep improving team communication?
<--- Score

46. Can you integrate quality management and risk management?
<--- Score

47. Are risk management tasks balanced centrally and locally?
<--- Score

48. How are team communication risks managed?
<--- Score

49. How do you define the solutions' scope?
<--- Score

50. Are decisions made in a timely manner?
<--- Score

51. How does your organization evaluate strategic team communication success?
<--- Score

52. Who will be responsible for documenting the team communication requirements in detail?
<--- Score

53. Are events managed to resolution?
<--- Score

54. How do you manage team communication risk?
<--- Score

55. What tools were used to tap into the creativity and encourage 'outside the box' thinking?
<--- Score

56. Are the most efficient solutions problem-specific?
<--- Score

57. Which of the recognised risks out of all risks can be

most likely transferred?
<--- Score

58. Who controls the risk?
<--- Score

59. How can you improve team communication?
<--- Score

60. How are policy decisions made and where?
<--- Score

61. What communications are necessary to support
the implementation of the solution?
<--- Score

**62. How do you use collaboration tools to improve
team communication?**
<--- Score

63. Are procedures documented for managing team
communication risks?
<--- Score

64. Was a team communication charter developed?
<--- Score

65. Can you identify any significant risks or exposures
to team communication third- parties (vendors,
service providers, alliance partners etc) that concern
you?
<--- Score

66. Is the scope clearly documented?
<--- Score

67. What team communication improvements can be made?
<--- Score

68. How do you decide how much to remunerate an employee?
<--- Score

69. Who manages team communication risk?
<--- Score

70. How do you mitigate team communication risk?
<--- Score

71. What are your current levels and trends in key measures or indicators of workforce and leader development?
<--- Score

72. What does the 'should be' process map/design look like?
<--- Score

73. Is team communication documentation maintained?
<--- Score

74. What are the expected team communication results?
<--- Score

75. Are risk triggers captured?
<--- Score

76. What can you do to improve?
<--- Score

77. What to do with the results or outcomes of measurements?
<--- Score

78. What improvements have been achieved?
<--- Score

79. What should a proof of concept or pilot accomplish?
<--- Score

80. Risk factors: what are the characteristics of team communication that make it risky?
<--- Score

81. What assumptions are made about the solution and approach?
<--- Score

82. What tools do you use once you have decided on a team communication strategy and more importantly how do you choose?
<--- Score

83. What went well, what should change, what can improve?
<--- Score

84. Were any criteria developed to assist the team in testing and evaluating potential solutions?
<--- Score

85. Risk Identification: What are the possible risk events your organization faces in relation to team communication?

<--- Score

86. Who will be responsible for making the decisions to include or exclude requested changes once team communication is underway?
<--- Score

87. Is any team communication documentation required?
<--- Score

88. To what extent does management recognize team communication as a tool to increase the results?
<--- Score

89. How risky is your organization?
<--- Score

90. How will you know that you have improved?
<--- Score

91. Are you assessing team communication and risk?
<--- Score

92. Is there any other team communication solution?
<--- Score

93. Which team communication solution is appropriate?
<--- Score

94. What is team communication's impact on utilizing the best solution(s)?
<--- Score

95. How can the phases of team communication

development be identified?
<--- Score

96. For decision problems, how do you develop a decision statement?
<--- Score

97. Are the key business and technology risks being managed?
<--- Score

98. What are the team communication security risks?
<--- Score

99. How do you measure improved team communication service perception, and satisfaction?
<--- Score

100. Is the team communication solution sustainable?
<--- Score

101. What error proofing will be done to address some of the discrepancies observed in the 'as is' process?
<--- Score

102. How significant is the improvement in the eyes of the end user?
<--- Score

103. What is the implementation plan?
<--- Score

104. Is the measure of success for team communication understandable to a variety of people?
<--- Score

105. Who should make the team communication decisions?
<--- Score

106. What alternative responses are available to manage risk?
<--- Score

107. What are the implications of the one critical team communication decision 10 minutes, 10 months, and 10 years from now?
<--- Score

108. Would you develop a team communication Communication Strategy?
<--- Score

109. How do you measure risk?
<--- Score

110. Do you need to do a usability evaluation?
<--- Score

111. How do you improve your likelihood of success ?
<--- Score

112. Where do the team communication decisions reside?
< Score

113. Is the solution technically practical?
<--- Score

114. How is continuous improvement applied to risk management?

<--- Score

115. How do you deal with team communication risk?
<--- Score

116. Why improve in the first place?
<--- Score

117. Does a good decision guarantee a good outcome?
<--- Score

118. How scalable is your team communication solution?
<--- Score

119. Who are the team communication decision-makers?
<--- Score

120. How do you go about comparing team communication approaches/solutions?
<--- Score

121. Who do you report team communication results to?
<--- Score

122. Do you combine technical expertise with business knowledge and team communication Key topics include lifecycles, development approaches, requirements and how to make a business case?
<--- Score

123. What criteria will you use to assess your team communication risks?

<--- Score

124. Who makes the team communication decisions in your organization?
<--- Score

125. Who manages supplier risk management in your organization?
<--- Score

126. What is the risk?
<--- Score

127. What is the team's contingency plan for potential problems occurring in implementation?
<--- Score

128. Is the team communication risk managed?
<--- Score

129. What were the underlying assumptions on the cost-benefit analysis?
<--- Score

130. What is the magnitude of the improvements?
<--- Score

131. Was a pilot designed for the proposed solution(s)?
<--- Score

132. What needs improvement? Why?
<--- Score

133. Is there a high likelihood that any recommendations will achieve their intended results?

<--- Score

134. Is there a cost/benefit analysis of optimal solution(s)?
<--- Score

135. Who will be using the results of the measurement activities?
<--- Score

136. What resources are required for the improvement efforts?
<--- Score

137. How is knowledge sharing about risk management improved?
<--- Score

138. Do you cover the five essential competencies: Communication, Collaboration,Innovation, Adaptability, and Leadership that improve an organizations ability to leverage the new team communication in a volatile global economy?
<--- Score

139. How can you better manage risk?
<--- Score

140. Who are the key stakeholders for the team communication evaluation?
<--- Score

Add up total points for this section:
_ _ _ _ _ = Total points for this section

Divided by: _ _ _ _ _ _ (number of

statements answered) = _____
Average score for this section

Transfer your score to the team
communication Index at the beginning
of the Self-Assessment.

CRITERION #6: CONTROL:

INTENT: Implement the practical solution. Maintain the performance and correct possible complications.

In my belief, the answer to this question is clearly defined:

5 Strongly Agree

4 Agree

3 Neutral

2 Disagree

1 Strongly Disagree

1. Is the team communication test/monitoring cost justified?
<--- Score

2. Does team communication appropriately measure and monitor risk?
<--- Score

3. Is new knowledge gained imbedded in the

response plan?
<--- Score

4. Is there a control plan in place for sustaining improvements (short and long-term)?
<--- Score

5. Are pertinent alerts monitored, analyzed and distributed to appropriate personnel?
<--- Score

6. How do your controls stack up?
<--- Score

7. How do you establish and deploy modified action plans if circumstances require a shift in plans and rapid execution of new plans?
<--- Score

8. How is change control managed?
<--- Score

9. How will report readings be checked to effectively monitor performance?
<--- Score

10. Is a response plan established and deployed?
<--- Score

11. What can you control?
<--- Score

12. How will team communication decisions be made and monitored?
<--- Score

13. What is your theory of human motivation, and how does your compensation plan fit with that view?
<--- Score

14. Is reporting being used or needed?
<--- Score

15. How widespread is its use?
<--- Score

16. Does job training on the documented procedures need to be part of the process team's education and training?
<--- Score

17. Do the team communication decisions you make today help people and the planet tomorrow?
<--- Score

18. What is your plan to assess your security risks?
<--- Score

19. Is a response plan in place for when the input, process, or output measures indicate an 'out-of-control' condition?
<--- Score

20. How will the day-to-day responsibilities for monitoring and continual improvement be transferred from the improvement team to the process owner?
<--- Score

21. You may have created your quality measures at a time when you lacked resources, technology wasn't up to the required standard, or low service levels

were the industry norm. Have those circumstances changed?

<--- Score

22. What do your reports reflect?

<--- Score

23. Are the planned controls in place?

<--- Score

24. What key inputs and outputs are being measured on an ongoing basis?

<--- Score

25. Are you measuring, monitoring and predicting team communication activities to optimize operations and profitability, and enhancing outcomes?

<--- Score

26. What are customers monitoring?

<--- Score

27. Are suggested corrective/restorative actions indicated on the response plan for known causes to problems that might surface?

<--- Score

28. Who sets the team communication standards?

<--- Score

29. What are the known security controls?

<--- Score

30. Is there an action plan in case of emergencies?

<--- Score

31. Do you monitor the effectiveness of your team communication activities?
<--- Score

32. How will input, process, and output variables be checked to detect for sub-optimal conditions?
<--- Score

33. How do you plan on providing proper recognition and disclosure of supporting companies?
<--- Score

34. How do you select, collect, align, and integrate team communication data and information for tracking daily operations and overall organizational performance, including progress relative to strategic objectives and action plans?
<--- Score

35. Is there a standardized process?
<--- Score

36. Is there documentation that will support the successful operation of the improvement?
<--- Score

37. How likely is the current team communication plan to come in on schedule or on budget?
<--- Score

38. What do you measure to verify effectiveness gains?
<--- Score

39. Where do ideas that reach policy makers and planners as proposals for team communication

strengthening and reform actually originate?
<--- Score

40. Will any special training be provided for results interpretation?
<--- Score

41. Is there a transfer of ownership and knowledge to process owner and process team tasked with the responsibilities.
<--- Score

42. Are the team communication standards challenging?
<--- Score

43. How do controls support value?
<--- Score

44. What is the best design framework for team communication organization now that, in a post industrial-age if the top-down, command and control model is no longer relevant?
<--- Score

45. How do you spread information?
<--- Score

46. Do the viable solutions scale to future needs?
<--- Score

47. How might the group capture best practices and lessons learned so as to leverage improvements?
<--- Score

48. Who controls critical resources?

<--- Score

49. What adjustments to the strategies are needed?
<--- Score

50. What quality tools were useful in the control phase?
<--- Score

51. Will existing staff require re-training, for example, to learn new business processes?
<--- Score

52. Do you monitor the team communication decisions made and fine tune them as they evolve?
<--- Score

53. What should the next improvement project be that is related to team communication?
<--- Score

54. What are the performance and scale of the team communication tools?
<--- Score

55. Who is going to spread your message?
<--- Score

56. Are documented procedures clear and easy to follow for the operators?
<--- Score

57. What are the critical parameters to watch?
<--- Score

58. Act/Adjust: What Do you Need to Do Differently?

<--- Score

59. Who is the team communication process owner?
<--- Score

60. What are the key elements of your team communication performance improvement system, including your evaluation, organizational learning, and innovation processes?
<--- Score

61. What other systems, operations, processes, and infrastructures (hiring practices, staffing, training, incentives/rewards, metrics/dashboards/scorecards, etc.) need updates, additions, changes, or deletions in order to facilitate knowledge transfer and improvements?
<--- Score

62. What is the recommended frequency of auditing?
<--- Score

63. Are new process steps, standards, and documentation ingrained into normal operations?
<--- Score

64. What are your results for key measures or indicators of the accomplishment of your team communication strategy and action plans, including building and strengthening core competencies?
<--- Score

65. Does the team communication performance meet the customer's requirements?
<--- Score

66. Who has control over resources?
<--- Score

67. In the case of a team communication project, the criteria for the audit derive from implementation objectives, an audit of a team communication project involves assessing whether the recommendations outlined for implementation have been met, can you track that any team communication project is implemented as planned, and is it working?
<--- Score

68. Is there a recommended audit plan for routine surveillance inspections of team communication's gains?
<--- Score

69. What is the control/monitoring plan?
<--- Score

70. Does the response plan contain a definite closed loop continual improvement scheme (e.g., plan-do-check-act)?
<--- Score

71. Is there a team communication Communication plan covering who needs to get what information when?
<--- Score

72. How is team communication project cost planned, managed, monitored?
<--- Score

73. Are controls in place and consistently applied?
<--- Score

74. Has the team communication value of standards been quantified?
<--- Score

75. Can support from partners be adjusted?
<--- Score

76. Implementation Planning: is a pilot needed to test the changes before a full roll out occurs?
<--- Score

77. Does a troubleshooting guide exist or is it needed?
<--- Score

78. Have new or revised work instructions resulted?
<--- Score

79. How do senior leaders actions reflect a commitment to the organizations team communication values?
<--- Score

80. How will new or emerging customer needs/ requirements be checked/communicated to orient the process toward meeting the new specifications and continually reducing variation?
<--- Score

81. What do you stand for--and what are you against?
<--- Score

82. How do you encourage people to take control and responsibility?
<--- Score

83. How will the process owner verify improvement in present and future sigma levels, process capabilities?
<--- Score

84. Are there documented procedures?
<--- Score

85. Is knowledge gained on process shared and institutionalized?
<--- Score

86. Will the team be available to assist members in planning investigations?
<--- Score

87. Are the planned controls working?
<--- Score

88. How will the process owner and team be able to hold the gains?
<--- Score

89. Is there a documented and implemented monitoring plan?
<--- Score

90. How do you monitor usage and cost?
<--- Score

91. What other areas of the group might benefit from the team communication team's improvements, knowledge, and learning?
<--- Score

92. What team communication standards are applicable?

<--- Score

93. Are operating procedures consistent?
<--- Score

94. Who will be in control?
<--- Score

95. How do you plan for the cost of succession?
<--- Score

96. What should you measure to verify efficiency gains?
<--- Score

97. Against what alternative is success being measured?
<--- Score

98. How can you best use all of your knowledge repositories to enhance learning and sharing?
<--- Score

99. Has the improved process and its steps been standardized?
<--- Score

100. Will your goals reflect your program budget?
<--- Score

101. How will you measure your QA plan's effectiveness?
<--- Score

Add up total points for this section:
_ _ _ _ _ = Total points for this section

Divided by: _____ (number of
statements answered) = _____
Average score for this section

Transfer your score to the team
communication Index at the beginning
of the Self-Assessment.

CRITERION #7: SUSTAIN:

INTENT: Retain the benefits.

In my belief, the answer to this question is clearly defined:

5 Strongly Agree

4 Agree

3 Neutral

2 Disagree

1 Strongly Disagree

1. What you are going to do to affect the numbers?
<--- Score

2. How do you manage all the streams of cross-team communication?
<--- Score

3. Is team communication realistic, or are you setting yourself up for failure?
<--- Score

4. Who is responsible for ensuring appropriate resources (time, people and money) are allocated to team communication?
<--- Score

5. How do you set team communication stretch targets and how do you get people to not only participate in setting these stretch targets but also that they strive to achieve these?
<--- Score

6. How do senior leaders deploy your organizations vision and values through your leadership system, to the workforce, to key suppliers and partners, and to customers and other stakeholders, as appropriate?
<--- Score

7. Who do you want your customers to become?
<--- Score

8. What are the business goals team communication is aiming to achieve?
<--- Score

9. Are you maintaining a past–present–future perspective throughout the team communication discussion?
<--- Score

10. What relationships among team communication trends do you perceive?
<--- Score

11. How long will it take to change?
<--- Score

12. At what moment would you think; Will I get fired?
<--- Score

13. Who are your customers?
<--- Score

14. Do you have the right capabilities and capacities?
<--- Score

15. What is the funding source for this project?
<--- Score

16. What potential megatrends could make your business model obsolete?
<--- Score

17. Why will customers want to buy your organizations products/services?
<--- Score

18. How do you keep the momentum going?
<--- Score

19. Do you think team communication accomplishes the goals you expect it to accomplish?
<--- Score

20. What stupid rule would you most like to kill?
<--- Score

21. What is the recommended frequency of auditing?
<--- Score

22. How do you manage team communication Knowledge Management (KM)?
<--- Score

23. How is the team communication?
<--- Score

24. How will you know that the team communication project has been successful?
<--- Score

25. Think of your team communication project, what are the main functions?
<--- Score

26. How do you proactively clarify deliverables and team communication quality expectations?
<--- Score

27. What are specific team communication rules to follow?
<--- Score

28. What are strategies for increasing support and reducing opposition?
<--- Score

29. How important is team communication to the user organizations mission?
<--- Score

30. What is your team communication strategy?
<--- Score

31. What are you challenging?
<--- Score

32. Who are the key stakeholders?
<--- Score

33. What factors effect team communication?
<--- Score

34. What is the purpose of team communication in relation to the mission?
<--- Score

35. Are the criteria for selecting recommendations stated?
<--- Score

36. What should you stop doing?
<--- Score

37. How do you create buy-in?
<--- Score

38. Operational - will it work?
<--- Score

39. Who are four people whose careers you have enhanced?
<--- Score

40. Do you have past team communication successes?
<--- Score

41. What are the top 3 things at the forefront of your team communication agendas for the next 3 years?
<--- Score

42. Why is team communication important for you now?
<--- Score

43. What is the overall talent health of your organization as a whole at senior levels, and for each organization reporting to a member of the Senior Leadership Team?
<--- Score

44. What is your BATNA (best alternative to a negotiated agreement)?
<--- Score

45. Is it economical; do you have the time and money?
<--- Score

46. Is there any reason to believe the opposite of my current belief?
<--- Score

47. What new services of functionality will be implemented next with team communication ?
<--- Score

48. What have you done to protect your business from competitive encroachment?
<--- Score

49. What is your question? Why?
<--- Score

50. What is a feasible sequencing of reform initiatives over time?
<--- Score

51. What are the success criteria that will indicate that team communication objectives have been met and the benefits delivered?
<--- Score

52. How do you accomplish your long range team communication goals?

<--- Score

53. Is there a team communication system?

<--- Score

54. What are the primary modes of team communication?

<--- Score

55. What are internal and external team communication relations?

<--- Score

56. How will you insure seamless interoperability of team communication moving forward?

<--- Score

57. What is the overall business strategy?

<--- Score

58. What one word do you want to own in the minds of your customers, employees, and partners?

<--- Score

59. Who will provide the final approval of team communication deliverables?

<--- Score

60. Is your strategy driving your strategy? Or is the way in which you allocate resources driving your strategy?

<--- Score

61. What are your personal philosophies regarding team communication and how do they influence your work?
<--- Score

62. Can the schedule be done in the given time?
<--- Score

63. Who do you think the world wants your organization to be?
<--- Score

64. What are the barriers to increased team communication production?
<--- Score

65. Marketing budgets are tighter, consumers are more skeptical, and social media has changed forever the way we talk about team communication, how do you gain traction?
<--- Score

66. How will you motivate the stakeholders with the least vested interest?
<--- Score

67. Which individuals, teams or departments will be involved in team communication?
<--- Score

68. Why not do team communication?
<--- Score

69. What are the gaps in your knowledge and experience?
<--- Score

70. What is the kind of project structure that would be appropriate for your team communication project, should it be formal and complex, or can it be less formal and relatively simple?
<--- Score

71. Are you / should you be revolutionary or evolutionary?
<--- Score

72. Why should people listen to you?
<--- Score

73. What projects are going on in the organization today, and what resources are those projects using from the resource pools?
<--- Score

74. What counts that you are not counting?
<--- Score

75. Instead of going to current contacts for new ideas, what if you reconnected with dormant contacts-- the people you used to know? If you were going reactivate a dormant tie, who would it be?
<--- Score

76. If you got fired and a new hire took your place, what would she do different?
<--- Score

77. How are you doing compared to your industry?
<--- Score

78. What are current team communication

paradigms?
<--- Score

79. Which functions and people interact with the supplier and or customer?
<--- Score

80. If you find that you havent accomplished one of the goals for one of the steps of the team communication strategy, what will you do to fix it?
<--- Score

81. Is maximizing team communication protection the same as minimizing team communication loss?
<--- Score

82. What does your signature ensure?
<--- Score

83. Is the team communication organization completing tasks effectively and efficiently?
<--- Score

84. What have been your experiences in defining long range team communication goals?
<--- Score

85. What was the last experiment you ran?
<--- Score

86. When information truly is ubiquitous, when reach and connectivity are completely global, when computing resources are infinite, and when a whole new set of impossibilities are not only possible, but happening, what will that do to your business?
<--- Score

87. Who will determine interim and final deadlines?
<--- Score

88. How do you foster the skills, knowledge, talents, attributes, and characteristics you want to have?
<--- Score

89. If you were responsible for initiating and implementing major changes in your organization, what steps might you take to ensure acceptance of those changes?
<--- Score

90. What may be the consequences for the performance of an organization if all stakeholders are not consulted regarding team communication?
<--- Score

91. Are all key stakeholders present at all Structured Walkthroughs?
<--- Score

92. Do you feel that more should be done in the team communication area?
<--- Score

93. Political -is anyone trying to undermine this project?
<--- Score

94. Can you maintain your growth without detracting from the factors that have contributed to your success?
<--- Score

95. What is the estimated value of the project?
<--- Score

96. Who is responsible for errors?
<--- Score

97. What unique value proposition (UVP) do you offer?
<--- Score

98. If you had to rebuild your organization without any traditional competitive advantages (i.e., no killer technology, promising research, innovative product/ service delivery model, etcetera), how would your people have to approach their work and collaborate together in order to create the necessary conditions for success?
<--- Score

99. What happens at your organization when people fail?
<--- Score

100. If you weren't already in this business, would you enter it today? And if not, what are you going to do about it?
<--- Score

101. What are your most important goals for the strategic team communication objectives?
<--- Score

102. What is the source of the strategies for team communication strengthening and reform?
<--- Score

103. What is your formula for success in team

communication ?
<--- Score

104. Who do we want your customers to become?
<--- Score

105. What team communication modifications can you make work for you?
<--- Score

106. What could happen if you do not do it?
<--- Score

107. Who uses your product in ways you never expected?
<--- Score

108. How do you go about securing team communication?
<--- Score

109. What goals did you miss?
<--- Score

110. How do you track customer value, profitability or financial return, organizational success, and sustainability?
<--- Score

111. What happens if you do not have enough funding?
<--- Score

112. How do you deal with team communication changes?
<--- Score

113. What are the challenges?
<--- Score

114. Whom among your colleagues do you trust, and for what?
<--- Score

115. What did you miss in the interview for the worst hire you ever made?
<--- Score

116. Is team communication dependent on the successful delivery of a current project?
<--- Score

117. Is there a work around that you can use?
<--- Score

118. Who is responsible for team communication?
<--- Score

119. What trophy do you want on your mantle?
<--- Score

120. Who is on the team?
<--- Score

121. Is a team communication team work effort in place?
<--- Score

122. What are the potential basics of team communication fraud?
<--- Score

123. What management system can you use to leverage the team communication experience, ideas, and concerns of the people closest to the work to be done?
<--- Score

124. Who will be responsible for deciding whether team communication goes ahead or not after the initial investigations?
<--- Score

125. What are the short and long-term team communication goals?
<--- Score

126. What are the long-term team communication goals?
<--- Score

127. How do you govern and fulfill your societal responsibilities?
<--- Score

128. What is it like to work for you?
<--- Score

129. How do you ensure that implementations of team communication products are done in a way that ensures safety?
<--- Score

130. How do you listen to customers to obtain actionable information?
<--- Score

131. Who else should you help?

<--- Score

132. If your company went out of business tomorrow, would anyone who doesn't get a paycheck here care?
<--- Score

133. What would have to be true for the option on the table to be the best possible choice?
<--- Score

134. What is your competitive advantage?
<--- Score

135. What is the range of capabilities?
<--- Score

136. What will be the consequences to the stakeholder (financial, reputation etc) if team communication does not go ahead or fails to deliver the objectives?
<--- Score

137. Why is it important to have senior management support for a team communication project?
<--- Score

138. Whose voice (department, ethnic group, women, older workers, etc) might you have missed hearing from in your company, and how might you amplify this voice to create positive momentum for your business?
<--- Score

139. Which team communication goals are the most important?
<--- Score

140. Why do and why don't your customers like your organization?

<--- Score

141. Where can you break convention?

<--- Score

142. How do you maintain team communication's Integrity?

<--- Score

143. How do you transition from the baseline to the target?

<--- Score

144. What are you trying to prove to yourself, and how might it be hijacking your life and business success?

<--- Score

145. How do you engage the workforce, in addition to satisfying them?

<--- Score

146. Which models, tools and techniques are necessary?

<--- Score

147. What team communication skills are most important?

<--- Score

148. If you do not follow, then how to lead?

<--- Score

149. If your customer were your grandmother, would

you tell her to buy what you're selling?
<--- Score

150. Are the assumptions believable and achievable?
<--- Score

151. To whom do you add value?
<--- Score

152. In the past year, what have you done (or could you have done) to increase the accurate perception of your company/brand as ethical and honest?
<--- Score

153. What are the key enablers to make this team communication move?
<--- Score

154. How will you ensure you get what you expected?
<--- Score

155. Is your basic point _____ or _____?
<--- Score

156. What is the craziest thing you can do?
<--- Score

157. Who is the main stakeholder, with ultimate responsibility for driving team communication forward?
<--- Score

158. How is implementation research currently incorporated into each of your goals?
<--- Score

159. How do you know if you are successful?
<--- Score

160. What knowledge, skills and characteristics mark a good team communication project manager?
<--- Score

161. What is an unauthorized commitment?
<--- Score

162. What business benefits will team communication goals deliver if achieved?
<--- Score

163. What trouble can you get into?
<--- Score

164. Would you rather sell to knowledgeable and informed customers or to uninformed customers?
<--- Score

165. Will there be any necessary staff changes (redundancies or new hires)?
<--- Score

166. What would you recommend your friend do if he/she were facing this dilemma?
<--- Score

167. What must you excel at?
<--- Score

168. How do you provide a safe environment -physically and emotionally?
<--- Score

169. Who have you, as a company, historically been when you've been at your best?
<--- Score

170. Are assumptions made in team communication stated explicitly?
<--- Score

171. How do you make it meaningful in connecting team communication with what users do day-to-day?
<--- Score

172. Do you think you know, or do you know you know ?
<--- Score

173. What is something you believe that nearly no one agrees with you on?
<--- Score

174. In retrospect, of the projects that you pulled the plug on, what percent do you wish had been allowed to keep going, and what percent do you wish had ended earlier?
<--- Score

175. How do you keep records, of what?
<--- Score

Add up total points for this section:
_____ = Total points for this section

Divided by: _____ (number of statements answered) = _____
Average score for this section

Transfer your score to the team
communication Index at the beginning
of the Self-Assessment.

Team Communication and Managing Projects, Criteria for Project Managers:

1.0 Initiating Process Group: Team Communication

1. What are the tools and techniques to be used in each phase?

2. What input will you be required to provide the Team Communication project team?

3. Are stakeholders properly informed about the status of the Team Communication project?

4. If the risk event occurs, what will you do?

5. Measurable - are the targets measurable?

6. What do they need to know about the Team Communication project?

7. How well did the chosen processes fit the needs of the Team Communication project?

8. What business situation is being addressed?

9. Does the Team Communication project team have enough people to execute the Team Communication project plan?

10. What are the short and long term implications?

11. What were the challenges that you encountered during the execution of a previous Team Communication project that you would not want to repeat?

12. Which of six sigmas dmaic phases focuses on the measurement of internal process that affect factors that are critical to quality?

13. Contingency planning. if a risk event occurs, what will you do?

14. Do you know all the stakeholders impacted by the Team Communication project and what needs are?

15. When must it be done?

16. Are you just doing busywork to pass the time?

17. How well did you do?

18. Will the Team Communication project meet the client requirements, and will it achieve the business success criteria that justified doing the Team Communication project in the first place?

19. Do you know if the Team Communication project requires outside equipment or vendor resources?

20. Where must it be done?

1.1 Project Charter: Team Communication

21. When?

22. Strategic fit: what is the strategic initiative identifier for this Team Communication project?

23. Must Have?

24. Why use a Team Communication project charter?

25. Why is a Team Communication project Charter used?

26. Dependent Team Communication projects: what Team Communication projects must be underway or completed before this Team Communication project can be successful?

27. What are you trying to accomplish?

28. Is it an improvement over existing products?

29. What are the known stakeholder requirements?

30. Where does all this information come from?

31. What are some examples of a business case?

32. Are there special technology requirements?

33. Customer benefits: what customer requirements

does this Team Communication project address?

34. What is the most common tool for helping define the detail?

35. What are you striving to accomplish (measurable goal(s))?

36. What date will the task finish?

37. For whom?

38. What are the assumptions?

39. Who is the sponsor?

40. What are the constraints?

1.2 Stakeholder Register: Team Communication

41. Who is managing stakeholder engagement?

42. What opportunities exist to provide communications?

43. How will reports be created?

44. What are the major Team Communication project milestones requiring communications or providing communications opportunities?

45. How much influence do they have on the Team Communication project?

46. How should employers make voices heard?

47. Who wants to talk about Security?

48. Who are the stakeholders?

49. How big is the gap?

50. Is your organization ready for change?

51. What & Why?

52. What is the power of the stakeholder?

1.3 Stakeholder Analysis Matrix: Team Communication

53. Are the interests in line with the program objectives?

54. Environmental effects?

55. Will the impacts be local, national or international?

56. What is the range you need to look at?

57. Supporters; who are the supporters?

58. What do you Evaluate?

59. New markets, vertical, horizontal?

60. Morale, commitment, leadership?

61. Partnerships, agencies, distribution?

62. What is in it for you?

63. Competitors vulnerabilities?

64. Do the stakeholders goals and expectations support or conflict with the Team Communication project goals?

65. Who will promote/support the Team Communication project, provided that they are involved?

66. Who will be affected by the work?

67. Which resources are required?

68. Information and research?

69. Guiding question: who shall you involve in the making of the stakeholder map?

70. Market demand?

71. How are the threatened Team Communication project targets being used?

2.0 Planning Process Group: Team Communication

72. What makes your Team Communication project successful?

73. Is the Team Communication project making progress in helping to achieve the set results?

74. Is the duration of the program sufficient to ensure a cycle that will Team Communication project the sustainability of the interventions?

75. What types of differentiated effects are resulting from the Team Communication project and to what extent?

76. Is the pace of implementing the products of the program ensuring the completeness of the results of the Team Communication project?

77. How are the principles of aid effectiveness (ownership, alignment, management for development results and mutual responsibility) being applied in the Team Communication project?

78. What are the different approaches to building the WBS?

79. Is the identification of the problems, inequalities and gaps, with respective causes, clear in the Team Communication project?

80. How do you integrate Team Communication project Planning with the Iterative/Evolutionary SDLC?

81. Who are the Team Communication project stakeholders?

82. Professionals want to know what is expected from them; what are the deliverables?

83. The Team Communication project charter is created in which Team Communication project management process group?

84. Does it make any difference if you are successful?

85. If you are late, will anybody notice?

86. Team Communication project assessment; why did you do this Team Communication project?

87. To what extent do the intervention objectives and strategies of the Team Communication project respond to your organizations plans?

88. You did your readings, yes?

89. How well do the team follow the chosen processes?

90. To what extent have the target population and participants made the activities own, taking an active role in it?

91. How will you know you did it?

2.1 Project Management Plan: Team Communication

92. What is risk management?

93. Do the proposed changes from the Team Communication project include any significant risks to safety?

94. If the Team Communication project management plan is a comprehensive document that guides you in Team Communication project execution and control, then what should it NOT contain?

95. What is the justification?

96. Development trends and opportunities. What if the positive direction and vision of your organization causes expected trends to change?

97. Has the selected plan been formulated using cost effectiveness and incremental analysis techniques?

98. What does management expect of PMs?

99. Who manages integration?

100. Are there any Client staffing expectations?

101. Are there any scope changes proposed for a previously authorized Team Communication project?

102. If the Team Communication project is complex or

scope is specialized, do you have appropriate and/or qualified staff available to perform the tasks?

103. What are the training needs?

104. What is the business need?

105. When is the Team Communication project management plan created?

106. Does the implementation plan have an appropriate division of responsibilities?

107. Is mitigation authorized or recommended?

2.2 Scope Management Plan: Team Communication

108. Does the Team Communication project team have the skills necessary to successfully complete current Team Communication project(s) and support the application?

109. Does the business case include how the Team Communication project aligns with your organizations strategic goals & objectives?

110. Is quality monitored from the perspective of the customers needs and expectations?

111. Has your organization readiness assessment been conducted?

112. Has stakeholder analysis been conducted, assessing influence on the Team Communication project and authority levels?

113. Are procurement deliverables arriving on time and to specification?

114. Is there general agreement & acceptance of the current status and progress of the Team Communication project?

115. Describe how the deliverables will be verified against the Team Communication project scope. To whom will the deliverables be first presented for inspection and verification?

116. Where do scope management processes fit in?

117. Does the Team Communication project have a Statement of Work?

118. What happens to rejected deliverables?

119. Have Team Communication project success criteria been defined?

120. Is each item clearly and completely defined?

121. Is the quality assurance team identified?

122. Are vendor contract reports, reviews and visits conducted periodically?

123. Are meeting minutes captured and sent out after the meeting?

124. Have stakeholder accountabilities & responsibilities been clearly defined?

125. Deliverables -are the deliverables tangible and verifiable?

2.3 Requirements Management Plan: Team Communication

126. Who will do the reporting and to whom will reports be delivered?

127. Has the requirements team been instructed in the Change Control process?

128. When and how will a requirements baseline be established in this Team Communication project?

129. Why manage requirements?

130. What are you counting on?

131. What went wrong?

132. Did you provide clear and concise specifications?

133. Who has the authority to reject Team Communication project requirements?

134. What cost metrics will be used?

135. How will bidders price evaluations be done, by deliverables, phases, or in a big bang?

136. What is a problem?

137. If it exists, where is it housed?

138. Are all the stakeholders ready for the transition

into the user community?

139. Do you have an agreed upon process for alerting the Team Communication project Manager if a request for change in requirements leads to a product scope change?

140. Did you get proper approvals?

141. Controlling Team Communication project requirements involves monitoring the status of the Team Communication project requirements and managing changes to the requirements. Who is responsible for monitoring and tracking the Team Communication project requirements?

142. Is infrastructure setup part of your Team Communication project?

143. Are actual resources expenditures versus planned expenditures acceptable?

144. Will you use an assessment of the Team Communication project environment as a tool to discover risk to the requirements process?

145. Business analysis scope?

2.4 Requirements Documentation: Team Communication

146. How much does requirements engineering cost?

147. How will requirements be documented and who signs off on them?

148. What is effective documentation?

149. Do your constraints stand?

150. What can tools do for us?

151. Can you check system requirements?

152. Is your business case still valid?

153. Are there any requirements conflicts?

154. Is the origin of the requirement clearly stated?

155. What are the acceptance criteria?

156. Consistency. are there any requirements conflicts?

157. How does what is being described meet the business need?

158. The problem with gathering requirements is right there in the word gathering. What images does it conjure?

159. What is a show stopper in the requirements?

160. What are the potential disadvantages/ advantages?

161. Is new technology needed?

162. Do technical resources exist?

163. Are all functions required by the customer included?

164. Who provides requirements?

165. What if the system wasn t implemented?

2.5 Requirements Traceability Matrix: Team Communication

166. Describe the process for approving requirements so they can be added to the traceability matrix and Team Communication project work can be performed. Will the Team Communication project requirements become approved in writing?

167. How small is small enough?

168. Why do you manage scope?

169. Is there a requirements traceability process in place?

170. Why use a WBS?

171. What percentage of Team Communication projects are producing traceability matrices between requirements and other work products?

172. Do you have a clear understanding of all subcontracts in place?

173. What is the WBS?

174. How do you manage scope?

175. Will you use a Requirements Traceability Matrix?

176. How will it affect the stakeholders personally in career?

177. What are the chronologies, contingencies, consequences, criteria?

2.6 Project Scope Statement: Team Communication

178. Elements that deal with providing the detail?

179. Will an issue form be in use?

180. Is the scope of your Team Communication project well defined?

181. Have you been able to thoroughly document the Team Communication projects assumptions and constraints?

182. Is there an information system for the Team Communication project?

183. Is the Team Communication project manager qualified and experienced in Team Communication project management?

184. Is your organization structure appropriate for the Team Communication projects size and complexity?

185. Is the Team Communication project organization documented and on file?

186. What went right?

187. How will you verify the accuracy of the work of the Team Communication project, and what constitutes acceptance of the deliverables?

188. What are the defined meeting materials?

189. Is the change control process documented and on file?

190. Has the format for tracking and monitoring schedules and costs been defined?

191. Elements of scope management that deal with concept development ?

192. Is the Team Communication project sponsor function identified and defined?

193. Are there completion/verification criteria defined for each task producing an output?

194. Is there a process (test plans, inspections, reviews) defined for verifying outputs for each task?

195. Are there adequate Team Communication project control systems?

196. Will the risk plan be updated on a regular and frequent basis?

2.7 Assumption and Constraint Log: Team Communication

197. Would known impacts serve as impediments?

198. Are there ways to reduce the time it takes to get something approved?

199. What strengths do you have?

200. How do you design an auditing system?

201. Diagrams and tables are included to account for complex concepts and increase overall readability?

202. Have all involved stakeholders and work groups committed to the Team Communication project?

203. Have the scope, objectives, costs, benefits and impacts been communicated to all involved and/or impacted stakeholders and work groups?

204. Security analysis has access to information that is sanitized?

205. Is the steering committee active in Team Communication project oversight?

206. Does the plan conform to standards?

207. What is positive about the current process?

208. What do you audit?

209. If appropriate, is the deliverable content consistent with current Team Communication project documents and in compliance with the Document Management Plan?

210. Is this model reasonable?

211. Does the system design reflect the requirements?

212. Is the current scope of the Team Communication project substantially different than that originally defined in the approved Team Communication project plan?

213. Are there processes defining how software will be developed including development methods, overall timeline for development, software product standards, and traceability?

214. What does an audit system look like?

215. Is the definition of the Team Communication project scope clear; what needs to be accomplished?

216. What other teams / processes would be impacted by changes to the current process, and how?

2.8 Work Breakdown Structure: Team Communication

217. How big is a work-package?

218. Where does it take place?

219. Is it a change in scope?

220. Why would you develop a Work Breakdown Structure?

221. When do you stop?

222. What is the probability of completing the Team Communication project in less that xx days?

223. When does it have to be done?

224. How will you and your Team Communication project team define the Team Communication projects scope and work breakdown structure?

225. How much detail?

226. Is the work breakdown structure (wbs) defined and is the scope of the Team Communication project clear with assigned deliverable owners?

227. How many levels?

228. When would you develop a Work Breakdown Structure?

229. What has to be done?

230. Is it still viable?

231. Why is it useful?

232. Can you make it?

233. Who has to do it?

2.9 WBS Dictionary: Team Communication

234. What should you drop in order to add something new?

235. Are meaningful indicators identified for use in measuring the status of cost and schedule performance?

236. Is the work done on a work package level as described in the WBS dictionary?

237. Are records maintained to show how undistributed budgets are controlled?

238. Are procedures established to prevent changes to the contract budget base other than the already stated authorized by contractual action?

239. Are overhead cost budgets established for each organization which has authority to incur overhead costs?

240. What is wrong with this Team Communication project?

241. Where learning is used in developing underlying budgets is there a direct relationship between anticipated learning and time phased budgets?

242. Is work properly classified as measured effort, LOE, or apportioned effort and appropriately

separated?

243. Contemplated overhead expenditure for each period based on the best information currently available?

244. Is future work which cannot be planned in detail subdivided to the extent practicable for budgeting and scheduling purposes?

245. All cwbs elements specified for external reporting?

246. Should you have a test for each code module?

247. Are overhead cost budgets (or Team Communication projections) established on a facility-wide basis at least annually for the life of the contract?

248. Are indirect costs accumulated for comparison with the corresponding budgets?

249. Are all affected work authorizations, budgeting, and scheduling documents amended to properly reflect the effects of authorized changes?

250. Can the contractor substantiate work package and planning package budgets?

251. Are retroactive changes to direct costs and indirect costs prohibited except for the correction of errors and routine accounting adjustments?

252. Does the scheduling system provide for the identification of work progress against technical and other milestones, and also provide for forecasts of

completion dates of scheduled work?

2.10 Schedule Management Plan: Team Communication

253. Has a sponsor been identified?

254. What is the difference between % Complete and % work?

255. Are the quality tools and methods identified in the Quality Plan appropriate to the Team Communication project?

256. Is the critical path valid?

257. Is it standard practice to formally commit stakeholders to the Team Communication project via agreements?

258. Is the schedule feasible and at what cost?

259. Has process improvement efforts been completed before requirements efforts begin?

260. Are risk triggers captured?

261. Are metrics used to evaluate and manage Vendors?

262. Is there any form of automated support for Issues Management?

263. Is documentation created for communication with the suppliers and Vendors?

264. Are schedule performance measures defined including pre-set triggers for specific actions?

265. Does the resource management plan include a personnel development plan?

266. Is there an onboarding process in place?

267. Has the schedule been baselined?

268. Is there an excessive and invalid use of task constraints and relationships of leads/lags?

269. Are software metrics formally captured, analyzed and used as a basis for other Team Communication project estimates?

270. Goal: is the schedule feasible and at what cost?

271. Have Team Communication project management standards and procedures been identified / established and documented?

2.11 Activity List: Team Communication

272. What went well?

273. How should ongoing costs be monitored to try to keep the Team Communication project within budget?

274. What did not go as well?

275. How will it be performed?

276. The wbs is developed as part of a joint planning session. and how do you know that youhave done this right?

277. Where will it be performed?

278. Should you include sub-activities?

279. What is the probability the Team Communication project can be completed in xx weeks?

280. In what sequence?

281. Can you determine the activity that must finish, before this activity can start?

282. Is there anything planned that does not need to be here?

283. What is the LF and LS for each activity?

284. How difficult will it be to do specific activities on this Team Communication project?

285. What is the total time required to complete the Team Communication project if no delays occur?

286. When do the individual activities need to start and finish?

287. What is your organizations history in doing similar activities?

288. What will be performed?

289. Are the required resources available or need to be acquired?

2.12 Activity Attributes: Team Communication

290. What is missing?

291. Resource is assigned to?

292. Can you re-assign any activities to another resource to resolve an over-allocation?

293. How else could the items be grouped?

294. Why?

295. How much activity detail is required?

296. Have constraints been applied to the start and finish milestones for the phases?

297. How difficult will it be to complete specific activities on this Team Communication project?

298. Would you consider either of corresponding activities an outlier?

299. What conclusions/generalizations can you draw from this?

300. What is the general pattern here?

301. Activity: what is In the Bag?

302. Does your organization of the data change its

meaning?

303. Where else does it apply?

304. Can more resources be added?

305. How difficult will it be to do specific activities on this Team Communication project?

2.13 Milestone List: Team Communication

306. Reliability of data, plan predictability?

307. Competitive advantages?

308. What are your competitors vulnerabilities?

309. How soon can the activity start?

310. Political effects?

311. Describe the industry you are in and the market growth opportunities. What is the market for your technology, product or service?

312. Timescales, deadlines and pressures?

313. Marketing - reach, distribution, awareness?

314. Calculate how long can activity be delayed?

315. Milestone pages should display the UserID of the person who added the milestone. Does a report or query exist that provides this audit information?

316. Loss of key staff?

317. What has been done so far?

318. Sustainable financial backing?

319. Global influences?

320. How will you get the word out to customers?

321. How soon can the activity finish?

322. What background experience, skills, and strengths does the team bring to your organization?

323. How difficult will it be to do specific activities on this Team Communication project?

2.14 Network Diagram: Team Communication

324. What are the Major Administrative Issues?

325. What controls the start and finish of a job?

326. Are the gantt chart and/or network diagram updated periodically and used to assess the overall Team Communication project timetable?

327. What activity must be completed immediately before this activity can start?

328. How difficult will it be to do specific activities on this Team Communication project?

329. What job or jobs follow it?

330. How confident can you be in your milestone dates and the delivery date?

331. What activities must follow this activity?

332. What job or jobs precede it?

333. What is the probability of completing the Team Communication project in less that xx days?

334. If a current contract exists, can you provide the vendor name, contract start, and contract expiration date?

335. What are the tools?

336. What can be done concurrently?

337. Why must you schedule milestones, such as reviews, throughout the Team Communication project?

338. Which type of network diagram allows you to depict four types of dependencies?

339. If x is long, what would be the completion time if you break x into two parallel parts of y weeks and z weeks?

340. What is the completion time?

341. What job or jobs could run concurrently?

342. Review the logical flow of the network diagram. Take a look at which activities you have first and then sequence the activities. Do they make sense?

2.15 Activity Resource Requirements: Team Communication

343. Why do you do that?

344. Organizational Applicability?

345. Other support in specific areas?

346. How many signatures do you require on a check and does this match what is in your policy and procedures?

347. Do you use tools like decomposition and rolling-wave planning to produce the activity list and other outputs?

348. How do you manage time?

349. What are constraints that you might find during the Human Resource Planning process?

350. Which logical relationship does the PDM use most often?

351. Time for overtime?

352. When does monitoring begin?

353. What is the Work Plan Standard?

354. How do you handle petty cash?

355. Are there unresolved issues that need to be addressed?

356. Anything else?

2.16 Resource Breakdown Structure: Team Communication

357. What are the requirements for resource data?

358. Who will use the system?

359. Why do you do it?

360. Why time management?

361. Who is allowed to perform which functions?

362. What defines a successful Team Communication project?

363. The list could probably go on, but, the thing that you would most like to know is, How long & How much?

364. What can you do to improve productivity?

365. What defines a successful Team Communication project?

366. What is Team Communication project communication management?

367. What is each stakeholders desired outcome for the Team Communication project?

368. How difficult will it be to do specific activities on this Team Communication project?

369. What is the purpose of assigning and documenting responsibility?

370. Who will be used as a Team Communication project team member?

371. How can this help you with team building?

372. Changes based on input from stakeholders?

373. Is predictive resource analysis being done?

2.17 Activity Duration Estimates: Team Communication

374. Who will provide training for the new application?

375. What are the nine areas of expertise?

376. Describe Team Communication project integration management in your own words. How does Team Communication project integration management relate to the Team Communication project life cycle, stakeholders, and the other Team Communication project management knowledge areas?

377. Do procedures exist describing how the Team Communication project scope will be managed?

378. Does a process exist to determine which risk events to accept and which events to disregard?

379. What is the difference between using brainstorming and the Delphi technique for risk identification?

380. Is risk identification completed regularly throughout the Team Communication project?

381. What is wrong with this scenario?

382. Is a contract change control system defined to manage changes to contract terms and conditions?

383. Will outside resources be needed to help in its development?

384. Find an example of a contract for information technology services. Analyze the key features of the contract. What type of contract was used and why?

385. Are activity duration estimates documented?

386. Sigma Team Communication project?

387. Do you agree with the suggestions provided for improving Team Communication project communications?

388. Calculate the expected duration for an activity that has a most likely time of 3, a pessimistic time of 10, and a optimiztic time of 2?

389. Account for the make-or-buy process and how to perform the financial calculations involved in the process. What are the main types of contracts if you do decide to outsource?

390. Team Communication project manager has received activity duration estimates from his team. Which does one need in order to complete schedule development?

391. Does a process exist to determine the potential loss or gain if risk events occur?

392. Briefly summarize the work done by Maslow, Herzberg, McClellan, McGregor, Ouchi, Thamhain and Wilemon, and Covey. How do theories relate to Team

Communication project management?

393. What do corresponding sources say about Team
Communication project management?

2.18 Duration Estimating Worksheet: Team Communication

394. For other activities, how much delay can be tolerated?

395. Done before proceeding with this activity or what can be done concurrently?

396. Science = process: remember the scientific method?

397. Small or large Team Communication project?

398. Does the Team Communication project provide innovative ways for stakeholders to overcome obstacles or deliver better outcomes?

399. What work will be included in the Team Communication project?

400. What utility impacts are there?

401. When, then?

402. Value pocket identification & quantification what are value pockets?

403. Do any colleagues have experience with your organization and/or RFPs?

404. Why estimate time and cost?

405. What info is needed?

406. Is this operation cost effective?

407. What is the total time required to complete the Team Communication project if no delays occur?

408. Why estimate costs?

409. Can the Team Communication project be constructed as planned?

410. How should ongoing costs be monitored to try to keep the Team Communication project within budget?

411. Will the Team Communication project collaborate with the local community and leverage resources?

412. Is a construction detail attached (to aid in explanation)?

2.19 Project Schedule: Team Communication

413. What does that mean?

414. How effectively were issues able to be resolved without impacting the Team Communication project Schedule or Budget?

415. Why do you need schedules?

416. How do you manage Team Communication project Risk?

417. Have all Team Communication project delays been adequately accounted for, communicated to all stakeholders and adjustments made in overall Team Communication project schedule?

418. What is risk?

419. Change management required?

420. What is the purpose of a Team Communication project schedule?

421. Are key risk mitigation strategies added to the Team Communication project schedule?

422. Verify that the update is accurate. Are all remaining durations correct?

423. Why do you think schedule issues often cause the

most conflicts on Team Communication projects?

424. What documents, if any, will the subcontractor provide (eg Team Communication project schedule, quality plan etc)?

425. How can you minimize or control changes to Team Communication project schedules?

426. Meet requirements?

427. How can slack be negative?

428. Are the original Team Communication project schedule and budget realistic?

429. What is the difference?

430. What is the most mis-scheduled part of process?

2.20 Cost Management Plan: Team Communication

431. Is the steering committee active in Team Communication project oversight?

432. Will the earned value reporting interface between time and cost management?

433. Are key risk mitigation strategies added to the Team Communication project schedule?

434. Pareto diagrams, statistical sampling, flow charting or trend analysis used quality monitoring?

435. How relevant is this attribute to this Team Communication project or audit?

436. Are tasks tracked by hours?

437. Is it possible to track all classes of Team Communication project work (e.g. scheduled, un-scheduled, defect repair, etc.)?

438. Are the schedule estimates reasonable given the Team Communication project?

439. Will the forecasts be based on trend analysis and earned value statistics?

440. Is an industry recognized mechanized support tool(s) being used for Team Communication project scheduling & tracking?

441. Are Team Communication project leaders committed to this Team Communication project full time?

442. What is Team Communication project management?

443. Schedule variances – how will schedule variances be identified and corrected?

444. What would the life cycle costs be?

445. Are cause and effect determined for risks when others occur?

446. Do Team Communication project managers participating in the Team Communication project know the Team Communication projects true status first hand?

2.21 Activity Cost Estimates: Team Communication

447. Maintenance Reserve?

448. What procedures are put in place regarding bidding and cost comparisons, if any?

449. Where can you get activity reports?

450. How do you do activity recasts?

451. Are cost subtotals needed?

452. Eac -estimate at completion, what is the total job expected to cost?

453. Does the activity rely on a common set of tools to carry it out?

454. What are the audit requirements?

455. Were sponsors and decision makers available when needed outside regularly scheduled meetings?

456. How quickly can the task be done with the skills available?

457. What is the Team Communication projects sustainability strategy that will ensure Team Communication project results will endure or be sustained?

458. If you are asked to lower your estimate because the price is too high, what are your options?

459. Why do you manage cost?

460. What is a Team Communication project Management Plan?

461. What is the estimators estimating history?

462. How Award?

463. Vac -variance at completion, how much over/ under budget do you expect to be?

464. Does the activity use a common approach or business function to deliver its results?

465. Does the estimator estimate by task or by person?

466. Certification of actual expenditures?

2.22 Cost Estimating Worksheet: Team Communication

467. What happens to any remaining funds not used?

468. Who is best positioned to know and assist in identifying corresponding factors?

469. What will others want?

470. What can be included?

471. What additional Team Communication project(s) could be initiated as a result of this Team Communication project?

472. Does the Team Communication project provide innovative ways for stakeholders to overcome obstacles or deliver better outcomes?

473. What costs are to be estimated?

474. Is the Team Communication project responsive to community need?

475. Ask: are others positioned to know, are others credible, and will others cooperate?

476. Is it feasible to establish a control group arrangement?

477. Can a trend be established from historical performance data on the selected measure and are

the criteria for using trend analysis or forecasting methods met?

478. How will the results be shared and to whom?

479. Will the Team Communication project collaborate with the local community and leverage resources?

480. Identify the timeframe necessary to monitor progress and collect data to determine how the selected measure has changed?

481. What is the estimated labor cost today based upon this information?

482. What is the purpose of estimating?

2.23 Cost Baseline: Team Communication

483. What do you want to measure ?

484. What is your organizations history in doing similar tasks?

485. How long are you willing to wait before you find out were late?

486. Have all the product or service deliverables been accepted by the customer?

487. On time?

488. What is the consequence?

489. Is the cr within Team Communication project scope?

490. Have all approved changes to the schedule baseline been identified and impact on the Team Communication project documented?

491. How concrete were original objectives?

492. Team Communication project goals -should others be reconsidered?

493. Will the Team Communication project fail if the change request is not executed?

494. Has operations management formally accepted responsibility for operating and maintaining the product(s) or service(s) delivered by the Team Communication project?

495. Have the actual milestone completion dates been compared to the approved schedule?

496. Does the suggested change request seem to represent a necessary enhancement to the product?

497. How do you manage cost?

498. Has the actual cost of the Team Communication project (or Team Communication project phase) been tallied and compared to the approved budget?

499. What deliverables come first?

2.24 Quality Management Plan: Team Communication

500. What worked well?

501. What is quality planning ?

502. How do senior leaders create and communicate values and performance expectations?

503. What data do you gather/use/compile?

504. Are you meeting the quality standards?

505. Written by multiple authors and in multiple writing styles?

506. Have all stakeholders been identified?

507. How do you decide what information to record?

508. How does your organization establish and maintain customer relationships?

509. How does your organization manage work to promote cooperation, individual initiative, innovation, flexibility, communications, and knowledge/skill sharing across work units?

510. Are there unnecessary steps that are creating bottlenecks and/or causing people to wait?

511. Is a component/condition present?

512. How are changes recorded?

513. How is staff trained in procedures?

514. What methods are used?

515. How is staff trained?

516. Documented results available?

517. Meet how often?

518. How does your organization address regulatory, legal, and ethical compliance?

519. How does your organization decide what to measure?

2.25 Quality Metrics: Team Communication

520. Why is now the time for quality metrics?

521. How do you measure?

522. Can visual measures help you to filter visualizations of interest?

523. When is the security analysis testing complete?

524. Is there a set of procedures to capture, analyze and act on quality metrics?

525. Can you correlate your quality metrics to profitability?

526. Are there already quality metrics available that detect nonlinear embeddings and trends similar to the users perception?

527. Are quality metrics defined?

528. Which are the right metrics to use?

529. If the defect rate during testing is substantially higher than that of the previous release (or a similar product), then ask: Did you plan for and actually improve testing effectiveness?

530. Is there alignment within your organization on definitions?

531. How exactly do you define when differences exist?

532. What metrics do you measure?

533. What is the CMS Benchmark?

534. What documentation is required?

535. Has it met internal or external standards?

536. The metrics–what is being considered?

537. How do you know if everyone is trying to improve the right things?

2.26 Process Improvement Plan: Team Communication

538. What is the test-cycle concept?

539. Has the time line required to move measurement results from the points of collection to databases or users been established?

540. Purpose of goal: the motive is determined by asking, why do you want to achieve this goal?

541. What personnel are the sponsors for that initiative?

542. Are there forms and procedures to collect and record the data?

543. Has a process guide to collect the data been developed?

544. What makes people good SPI coaches?

545. Where do you want to be?

546. To elicit goal statements, do you ask a question such as, What do you want to achieve?

547. Modeling current processes is great, and will you ever see a return on that investment?

548. Does your process ensure quality?

549. What personnel are the champions for the initiative?

550. Are you making progress on the goals?

551. What is the return on investment?

552. Does explicit definition of the measures exist?

553. What personnel are the coaches for your initiative?

2.27 Responsibility Assignment Matrix: Team Communication

554. Identify potential or actual budget-based and time-based schedule variances?

555. Is the entire contract planned in time-phased control accounts to the extent practicable?

556. Are material costs reported within the same period as that in which BCWP is earned for that material?

557. Are control accounts opened and closed based on the start and completion of work contained therein?

558. Is cost and schedule performance measurement done in a consistent, systematic manner?

559. Actual cost of work performed?

560. Team Communication projected economic escalation?

561. What happens when others get pulled for higher priority Team Communication projects?

562. Incurrence of actual indirect costs in excess of budgets, by element of expense?

563. What simple tool can you use to help identify and prioritize Team Communication project risks that is

very low tech and high touch?

564. Changes in the direct base to which overhead costs are allocated?

565. The anticipated business volume?

566. Evaluate the performance of operating organizations?

567. Are data elements reconcilable between internal summary reports and reports forwarded to stakeholders?

568. Does the contractor use objective results, design reviews and tests to trace schedule performance?

569. Budgeted cost for work scheduled?

570. Are records maintained to show how management reserves are used?

571. Who is responsible for work and budgets for each wbs?

572. Time-phased control account budgets?

2.28 Roles and Responsibilities: Team Communication

573. Was the expectation clearly communicated?

574. What should you highlight for improvement?

575. What expectations were met?

576. Who is responsible for implementation activities and where will the functions, roles and responsibilities be defined?

577. What are your major roles and responsibilities in the area of performance measurement and assessment?

578. Do the values and practices inherent in the culture of your organization foster or hinder the process?

579. Have you ever been a part of this team?

580. Are governance roles and responsibilities documented?

581. Are Team Communication project team roles and responsibilities identified and documented?

582. What areas of supervision are challenging for you?

583. Key conclusions and recommendations: Are

conclusions and recommendations relevant and acceptable?

584. Is feedback clearly communicated and non-judgmental?

585. Once the responsibilities are defined for the Team Communication project, have the deliverables, roles and responsibilities been clearly communicated to every participant?

586. What expectations were NOT met?

587. How well did the Team Communication project Team understand the expectations of specific roles and responsibilities?

588. What is working well within your organizations performance management system?

589. What should you do now to prepare yourself for a promotion, increased responsibilities or a different job?

590. What should you do now to ensure that you are meeting all expectations of your current position?

591. Authority: what areas/Team Communication projects in your work do you have the authority to decide upon and act on the already stated decisions?

592. Are Team Communication project team roles and responsibilities identified and documented?

2.29 Human Resource Management Plan: Team Communication

593. Are all key components of a Quality Assurance Plan present?

594. Were decisions made in a timely manner?

595. How are superior performers differentiated from average performers?

596. Does the detailed work plan match the complexity of tasks with the capabilities of personnel?

597. Is there a formal set of procedures supporting Stakeholder Management?

598. Was the scope definition used in task sequencing?

599. Have the key elements of a coherent Team Communication project management strategy been established?

600. Are Team Communication project contact logs kept up to date?

601. Is pert / critical path or equivalent methodology being used?

602. Do you have the reasons why the changes to your organizational systems and capabilities are required?

603. Is Team Communication project work proceeding in accordance with the original Team Communication project schedule?

604. Is there a requirements change management processes in place?

605. Were stakeholders aware and supportive of the principles and practices of modern cost estimation?

606. Are vendor invoices audited for accuracy before payment?

607. Is the structure for tracking the Team Communication project schedule well defined and assigned to a specific individual?

608. Is it possible to track all classes of Team Communication project work (e.g. scheduled, un-scheduled, defect repair, etc.)?

2.30 Communications Management Plan: Team Communication

609. Who is responsible?

610. Who to learn from?

611. Timing: when do the effects of the communication take place?

612. Are the stakeholders getting the information others need, are others consulted, are concerns addressed?

613. Are there too many who have an interest in some aspect of your work?

614. Are others part of the communications management plan?

615. What are the interrelationships?

616. What is the stakeholders level of authority?

617. Who will use or be affected by the result of a Team Communication project?

618. Do you have members of your team responsible for certain stakeholders?

619. In your work, how much time is spent on stakeholder identification?

620. Can you think of other people who might have concerns or interests?

621. How often do you engage with stakeholders?

622. Is there an important stakeholder who is actively opposed and will not receive messages?

623. Are others needed?

624. Which stakeholders can influence others?

625. Do you then often overlook a key stakeholder or stakeholder group?

626. Will messages be directly related to the release strategy or phases of the Team Communication project?

627. How did the term stakeholder originate?

2.31 Risk Management Plan: Team Communication

628. What risks are tracked?

629. Is security a central objective?

630. Do the people have the right combinations of skills?

631. Number of users of the product?

632. Are there risks to human health or the environment that need to be controlled or mitigated?

633. Risk categories: what are the main categories of risks that should be addressed on this Team Communication project?

634. Are the required plans included, such as nonstructural flood risk management plans?

635. Minimize cost and financial risk?

636. Is the customer willing to participate in reviews?

637. Does the customer have a solid idea of what is required?

638. What will drive change?

639. Are you working on the right risks?

640. How is risk identification performed?

641. What are it-specific requirements?

642. Have top software and customer managers formally committed to support the Team Communication project?

643. How quickly does each item need to be resolved?

644. Have staff received necessary training?

645. Can you stabilize dynamic risk factors?

646. What would you do?

647. Are tools for analysis and design available?

2.32 Risk Register: Team Communication

648. Can the likelihood and impact of failing to achieve corresponding recommendations and action plans be assessed?

649. What has changed since the last period?

650. Are corrective measures implemented as planned?

651. Cost/benefit – how much will the proposed mitigations cost and how does this cost compare with the potential cost of the risk event/situation should it occur?

652. When is it going to be done?

653. Risk probability and impact: how will the probabilities and impacts of risk items be assessed?

654. Technology risk -is the Team Communication project technically feasible?

655. Are there any gaps in the evidence?

656. Having taken action, how did the responses effect change, and where is the Team Communication project now?

657. What should you do when?

658. Amongst the action plans and recommendations that you have to introduce are there some that could stop or delay the overall program?

659. How well are risks controlled?

660. What risks might negatively or positively affect achieving the Team Communication project objectives?

661. How is a Community Risk Register created?

662. What would the impact to the Team Communication project objectives be should the risk arise?

663. Are implemented controls working as others should?

664. What further options might be available for responding to the risk?

665. What can be done about it?

666. What will be done?

2.33 Probability and Impact Assessment: Team Communication

667. Are the risk data complete?

668. What risks are necessary to achieve success?

669. Should the risk be taken at all?

670. Who will be responsible for a slippage?

671. Are the software tools integrated with each other?

672. What should be the external organizations responsibility vis-à-vis total stake in the Team Communication project?

673. What things are likely to change?

674. My Team Communication project leader has suddenly left your organization, what do you do?

675. Risk data quality assessment - what is the quality of the data used to determine or assess the risk?

676. Are end-users enthusiastically committed to the Team Communication project and the system/product to be built?

677. What should be done with non-critical risks?

678. Are trained personnel, including supervisors and

Team Communication project managers, available to handle such a large Team Communication project?

679. What are the likely future requirements?

680. How do you maximize short-term return on investment?

681. Are people attending meetings and doing work?

682. Are there alternative opinions/solutions/ processes you should explore?

683. Can the Team Communication project proceed without assuming the risk?

684. How are the local factors going to affect the absorption?

685. Do end-users have realistic expectations?

686. Have customers been involved fully in the definition of requirements?

2.34 Probability and Impact Matrix: Team Communication

687. Can you handle the investment risk?

688. Economic to take on the Team Communication project?

689. Were there any Team Communication projects similar to this one in existence?

690. Is the process supported by tools?

691. What are the methods to deal with risks?

692. Have you worked with the customer in the past?

693. Does the Team Communication project team have experience with the technology to be implemented?

694. Are enough people available?

695. Mitigation -how can you avoid the risk?

696. What is the likelihood?

697. What will be the likely political environment during the life of the Team Communication project?

698. What should be done NEXT?

699. What action would you take to the identified risks

in the Team Communication project?

700. Have you ascribed a level of confidence to every critical technical objective?

701. Can it be enlarged by drawing people from other areas of your organization?

702. Risk may be made during which step of risk management?

703. Risk categorization -which of your categories has more risk than others?

704. What would you do differently?

2.35 Risk Data Sheet: Team Communication

705. How do you handle product safely?

706. What were the Causes that contributed?

707. What do people affected think about the need for, and practicality of preventive measures?

708. What do you know?

709. What are you weak at and therefore need to do better?

710. Potential for recurrence?

711. What can happen?

712. Is the data sufficiently specified in terms of the type of failure being analyzed, and its frequency or probability?

713. Do effective diagnostic tests exist?

714. Are new hazards created?

715. What are you trying to achieve (Objectives)?

716. What are the main threats to your existence?

717. Has a sensitivity analysis been carried out?

718. How reliable is the data source?

719. What if client refuses?

720. Has the most cost-effective solution been chosen?

721. Whom do you serve (customers)?

722. Will revised controls lead to tolerable risk levels?

723. During work activities could hazards exist?

2.36 Procurement Management Plan: Team Communication

724. Do Team Communication project managers participating in the Team Communication project know the Team Communication projects true status first hand?

725. Does the Team Communication project have a Quality Culture?

726. Are the quality tools and methods identified in the Quality Plan appropriate to the Team Communication project?

727. Is it standard practice to formally commit stakeholders to the Team Communication project via agreements?

728. Is the structure for tracking the Team Communication project schedule well defined and assigned to a specific individual?

729. If standardized procurement documents are needed, where can others be found?

730. Are changes in scope (deliverable commitments) agreed to by all affected groups & individuals?

731. Are key risk mitigation strategies added to the Team Communication project schedule?

732. Is the communication plan being followed?

733. Are Team Communication project contact logs kept up to date?

734. How long will it take for the purchase cost to be the same as the lease cost?

735. Have key stakeholders been identified?

736. Were Team Communication project team members involved in the development of activity & task decomposition?

737. Public engagement – did you get it right?

738. Is the Team Communication project sponsor clearly communicating the business case or rationale for why this Team Communication project is needed?

739. Have adequate resources been provided by management to ensure Team Communication project success?

740. Is there a procurement management plan in place?

741. Are risk oriented checklists used during risk identification?

2.37 Source Selection Criteria: Team Communication

742. How do you ensure an integrated assessment of proposals?

743. What is the basis of an estimate and what assumptions were made?

744. Who is entitled to a debriefing?

745. What will you use to capture evaluation and subsequent documentation?

746. What common questions or problems are associated with debriefings?

747. Are considerations anticipated?

748. What can not be disclosed?

749. Do you consider all weaknesses, significant weaknesses, and deficiencies?

750. What should clarifications include?

751. What should be considered?

752. Which contract type places the most risk on the seller?

753. When and what information can be considered with offerors regarding past performance?

754. Is the offeror pricing what is technically proposed?

755. Do you want to wait until all offerors have been evaluated?

756. How should oral presentations be prepared for?

757. Does an evaluation need to include the identification of strengths and weaknesses?

758. When should debriefings be held and how should they be scheduled?

759. How should the oral presentations be handled?

760. What should communications be used to accomplish?

761. What procedures are followed when a contractor requires access to classified information or a significant quantity of special material/information?

2.38 Stakeholder Management Plan: Team Communication

762. What is the general purpose in defining responsibilities of the already stated affiliated with the Team Communication project?

763. Have all necessary approvals been obtained?

764. What methods are to be used for managing and monitoring subcontractors (eg agreements, contracts etc)?

765. Are there nonconformance issues?

766. Contradictory information between document sections?

767. Detail warranty and/or maintenance periods?

768. Are Team Communication project team members committed fulltime?

769. Are there any potential occupational health and safety issues due to the proposed purchases?

770. Are all payments made according to the contract(s)?

771. What are reporting requirements?

772. Has the Team Communication project scope been baselined?

773. Who will the report(s) be delivered to?

774. How are new requirements or changes to requirements identified?

775. What are the procedures and processes to be followed for purchases, including approval and authorisation requirements?

776. Does the role of the Team Communication project Team cease upon the delivery of the Team Communication projects outputs?

777. Are software metrics formally captured, analyzed and used as a basis for other Team Communication project estimates?

778. After observing execution of process, is it in compliance with the documented Plan?

779. Has the business need been clearly defined?

2.39 Change Management Plan: Team Communication

780. Where will the funds come from?

781. What does a resilient organization look like?

782. What is the most positive interpretation it can receive?

783. How badly can information be misinterpreted?

784. What are the current methods of sharing information and do there need to be new ones developed?

785. What is the most cynical response it can receive?

786. Impact of systems implementation on organization change?

787. What work practices will be affected?

788. Is it the same for each of the business units?

789. How do you gain sponsors buy-in to the communication plan?

790. Has a training need analysis been carried out?

791. How might they respond to the message and if the response may be negative or open to misinterpretation, what else needs to be said?

792. How far reaching in your organization is the change?

793. Change invariability confront many relationships especially the already stated that require a set of behaviours What roles with in your organization are affected and how?

794. What processes are in place to manage knowledge about the Team Communication project?

795. When does it make sense to customize?

796. What are the specific target groups/audiences that will be impacted by this change?

797. Who might be able to help you the most?

798. Has this been negotiated with the customer and sponsor?

3.0 Executing Process Group: Team Communication

799. What type of information goes in the quality assurance plan?

800. Is the program supported by national and/or local organizations?

801. Is the schedule for the set products being met?

802. Is the Team Communication project making progress in helping to achieve the set results?

803. Is activity definition the first process involved in Team Communication project time management?

804. Who will be the main sponsor?

805. In what way has the program come up with innovative measures for problem-solving?

806. What are the main processes included in Team Communication project quality management?

807. Do schedule issues conflicts?

808. What are the Team Communication project management deliverables of each process group?

809. What is involved in the solicitation process?

810. What are the critical steps involved in selecting

measures and initiatives?

811. Do the partners have sufficient financial capacity to keep up the benefits produced by the programme?

812. What areas does the group agree are the biggest success on the Team Communication project?

813. Do Team Communication project managers understand your organizational context for Team Communication projects?

814. What are the main parts of the scope statement?

815. If a risk event occurs, what will you do?

816. What are the key components of the Team Communication project communications plan?

817. What is in place for ensuring adequate change control on Team Communication projects that involve outside contracts?

818. What are deliverables of your Team Communication project?

3.1 Team Member Status Report: Team Communication

819. How it is to be done?

820. When a teams productivity and success depend on collaboration and the efficient flow of information, what generally fails them?

821. How can you make it practical?

822. How will resource planning be done?

823. What specific interest groups do you have in place?

824. The problem with Reward & Recognition Programs is that the truly deserving people all too often get left out. How can you make it practical?

825. How much risk is involved?

826. Are the attitudes of staff regarding Team Communication project work improving?

827. How does this product, good, or service meet the needs of the Team Communication project and your organization as a whole?

828. Does the product, good, or service already exist within your organization?

829. What is to be done?

830. Why is it to be done?

831. Are the products of your organizations Team Communication projects meeting customers objectives?

832. Is there evidence that staff is taking a more professional approach toward management of your organizations Team Communication projects?

833. Will the staff do training or is that done by a third party?

834. Are your organizations Team Communication projects more successful over time?

835. Do you have an Enterprise Team Communication project Management Office (EPMO)?

836. Does every department have to have a Team Communication project Manager on staff?

837. Does your organization have the means (staff, money, contract, etc.) to produce or to acquire the product, good, or service?

3.2 Change Request: Team Communication

838. Are you implementing itil processes?

839. What are the requirements for urgent changes?

840. Who is responsible to authorize changes?

841. Is it feasible to use requirements attributes as predictors of reliability?

842. Who is included in the change control team?

843. Will new change requests be acknowledged in a timely manner?

844. Should staff call into the helpdesk or go to the website?

845. Will the change use memory to the extent that other functions will be not have sufficient memory to operate effectively?

846. How are changes requested (forms, method of communication)?

847. How fast will change requests be approved?

848. Why do you want to have a change control system?

849. How can you ensure that changes have been

made properly?

850. What are the basic mechanics of the Change Advisory Board (CAB)?

851. Should a more thorough impact analysis be conducted?

852. Change request coordination ?

853. Since there are no change requests in your Team Communication project at this point, what must you have before you begin?

854. How can changes be graded?

855. Are there requirements attributes that are strongly related to the complexity and size?

856. Can you answer what happened, who did it, when did it happen, and what else will be affected?

857. How shall the implementation of changes be recorded?

3.3 Change Log: Team Communication

858. Does the suggested change request represent a desired enhancement to the products functionality?

859. Will the Team Communication project fail if the change request is not executed?

860. Is the submitted change a new change or a modification of a previously approved change?

861. Is the requested change request a result of changes in other Team Communication project(s)?

862. How does this change affect scope?

863. How does this change affect the timeline of the schedule?

864. Where do changes come from?

865. Do the described changes impact on the integrity or security of the system?

866. When was the request approved?

867. Is the change request within Team Communication project scope?

868. How does this relate to the standards developed for specific business processes?

869. Is the change backward compatible without limitations?

870. Is this a mandatory replacement?

871. Is the change request open, closed or pending?

872. When was the request submitted?

873. Who initiated the change request?

3.4 Decision Log: Team Communication

874. What is the average size of your matters in an applicable measurement?

875. Adversarial environment. is your opponent open to a non-traditional workflow, or will it likely challenge anything you do?

876. Is everything working as expected?

877. Behaviors; what are guidelines that the team has identified that will assist them with getting the most out of team meetings?

878. Who will be given a copy of this document and where will it be kept?

879. What is your overall strategy for quality control / quality assurance procedures?

880. What was the rationale for the decision?

881. With whom was the decision shared or considered?

882. Do strategies and tactics aimed at less than full control reduce the costs of management or simply shift the cost burden?

883. How do you define success?

884. Who is the decisionmaker?

885. Decision-making process; how will the team make decisions?

886. What is the line where eDiscovery ends and document review begins?

887. It becomes critical to track and periodically revisit both operational effectiveness; Are you noticing all that you need to, and are you interpreting what you see effectively?

888. Meeting purpose; why does this team meet?

889. Linked to original objective?

890. Is your opponent open to a non-traditional workflow, or will it likely challenge anything you do?

891. How does an increasing emphasis on cost containment influence the strategies and tactics used?

892. What makes you different or better than others companies selling the same thing?

893. How effective is maintaining the log at facilitating organizational learning?

3.5 Quality Audit: Team Communication

894. Are all records associated with the reconditioning of a device maintained for a minimum of two years after the sale or disposal of the last device within a lot of merchandise?

895. How does your organization know that its systems for communicating with and among staff are appropriately effective and constructive?

896. Are complaint files maintained?

897. How does your organization know that its system for ensuring that its training activities are appropriately resourced and support is appropriately effective and constructive?

898. Are training programs documented?

899. Are multiple statements on the same issue consistent with each other?

900. How does your organization know that its research planning and management systems are appropriately effective and constructive in enabling quality research outcomes?

901. Are the review comments incorporated?

902. Are salvageable and salvaged medical devices stored in a manner to prevent damage and/or

contamination?

903. What has changed/improved as a result of the review processes?

904. What experience do staff have in the type of work that the audit entails?

905. Will the evidence likely be sufficient and appropriate?

906. How does your organization ensure that equipment is appropriately maintained and producing valid results?

907. What review processes are in place for your organizations major activities?

908. Is your organizational structure established and each positions responsibility defined?

909. Is the process of self review, learning and improvement endemic throughout your organization?

910. How does your organization know that its financial management system is appropriately effective and constructive?

911. What data about organizational performance is routinely collected and reported?

912. Are goals well supported with strategies, operational plans, manuals and training?

913. Is progress against the intentions measurable?

3.6 Team Directory: Team Communication

914. How do unidentified risks impact the outcome of the Team Communication project?

915. How will you accomplish and manage the objectives?

916. Process decisions: do job conditions warrant additional actions to collect job information and document on-site activity?

917. Process decisions: how well was task order work performed?

918. Who are your stakeholders (customers, sponsors, end users, team members)?

919. Who will be the stakeholders on your next Team Communication project?

920. Who will write the meeting minutes and distribute?

921. Who will report Team Communication project status to all stakeholders?

922. Timing: when do the effects of communication take place?

923. Process decisions: are all start-up, turn over and close out requirements of the contract satisfied?

924. How does the team resolve conflicts and ensure tasks are completed?

925. Process decisions: is work progressing on schedule and per contract requirements?

926. When does information need to be distributed?

927. Days from the time the issue is identified?

928. Process decisions: are contractors adequately prosecuting the work?

929. Does a Team Communication project team directory list all resources assigned to the Team Communication project?

930. Have you decided when to celebrate the Team Communication projects completion date?

931. Where should the information be distributed?

932. Who are the Team Members?

3.7 Team Operating Agreement: Team Communication

933. How will you resolve conflict efficiently and respectfully?

934. Are leadership responsibilities shared among team members (versus a single leader)?

935. How do you want to be thought of and known within your organization?

936. Do you prevent individuals from dominating the meeting?

937. Have you set the goals and objectives of the team?

938. The method to be used in the decision making process; Will it be consensus, majority rule, or the supervisor having the final say?

939. Do you solicit member feedback about meetings and what would make them better?

940. Do you determine the meeting length and time of day?

941. To whom do you deliver your services?

942. Did you prepare participants for the next meeting?

943. Have you established procedures that team members can follow to work effectively together, such as a team operating agreement?

944. Has the appropriate access to relevant data and analysis capability been granted?

945. What is group supervision?

946. What are the current caseload numbers in the unit?

947. Are there more than two functional areas represented by your team?

948. Do you upload presentation materials in advance and test the technology?

949. What is your unique contribution to your organization?

950. Do team members need to frequently communicate as a full group to make timely decisions?

951. Are there influences outside the team that may affect performance, and if so, have you identified and addressed them?

952. What is the number of cases currently teamed?

3.8 Team Performance Assessment: Team Communication

953. If you have received criticism from reviewers that your work suffered from method variance, what was the circumstance?

954. Lack of method variance in self-reported affect and perceptions at work: Reality or artifact?

955. Individual task proficiency and team process behavior: what is important for team functioning?

956. Do you give group members authority to make at least some important decisions?

957. Social categorization and intergroup behaviour: Does minimal intergroup discrimination make social identity more positive?

958. Where to from here?

959. To what degree do team members articulate the teams work approach?

960. How hard did you try to make a good selection?

961. What is method variance?

962. To what degree are the members clear on what they are individually responsible for and what they are jointly responsible for?

963. To what degree do team members understand one anothers roles and skills?

964. To what degree are corresponding categories of skills either actually or potentially represented across the membership?

965. How does Team Communication project termination impact Team Communication project team members?

966. Delaying market entry: how long is too long?

967. To what degree will new and supplemental skills be introduced as the need is recognized?

968. If you have criticized someones work for method variance in your role as reviewer, what was the circumstance?

969. To what degree are the teams goals and objectives clear, simple, and measurable?

970. To what degree does the teams work approach provide opportunity for members to engage in fact-based problem solving?

971. Do friends perform better than acquaintances?

972. To what degree do team members feel that the purpose of the team is important, if not exciting?

3.9 Team Member Performance Assessment: Team Communication

973. How do you start collaborating?

974. How do you use data to inform instruction and improve staff achievement?

975. What are the key duties or tasks of the Ratee?

976. Which training platform formats (i.e., mobile, virtual, videogame-based) were implemented in your effort(s)?

977. To what degree are the relative importance and priority of the goals clear to all team members?

978. What are best practices for delivering and developing training evaluations to maximize the benefits of leveraging emerging technologies?

979. How is the timing of assessments organized (e.g., pre/post-test, single point during training, multiple reassessment during training)?

980. What are they responsible for?

981. Does platform-specific assessment information contribute to training placement or tailoring of instruction (e.g. aptitude-treatment interaction)?

982. How is your organizations Strategic Management System tied to performance measurement?

983. Is it critical or vital to the job?

984. What qualities does a successful Team leader possess?

985. To what degree does the teams approach to its work allow for modification and improvement over time?

986. What variables that affect team members achievement are within your control?

987. How should adaptive assessments be implemented?

988. To what extent are systems and applications (e.g., game engine, mobile device platform) utilized?

989. To what degree do all members feel responsible for all agreed-upon measures?

990. To what degree do team members frequently explore the teams purpose and its implications?

991. How often are assessments to be conducted?

992. What steps have you taken to improve performance?

3.10 Issue Log: Team Communication

993. What is a Stakeholder?

994. Which team member will work with each stakeholder?

995. Do you prepare stakeholder engagement plans?

996. What are the stakeholders interrelationships?

997. Persistence; will users learn a work around or will they be bothered every time?

998. How do you manage communications?

999. Who are the members of the governing body?

1000. How is this initiative related to other portfolios, programs, or Team Communication projects?

1001. What is the stakeholders political influence?

1002. What approaches to you feel are the best ones to use?

1003. Who is the issue assigned to?

1004. Are you constantly rushing from meeting to meeting?

1005. Can an impact cause deviation beyond team, stage or Team Communication project tolerances?

1006. What effort will a change need?

1007. Is the issue log kept in a safe place?

1008. Are stakeholder roles recognized by your organization?

4.0 Monitoring and Controlling Process Group: Team Communication

1009. Specific - is the objective clear in terms of what, how, when, and where the situation will be changed?

1010. Is the program making progress in helping to achieve the set results?

1011. What factors are contributing to progress or delay in the achievement of products and results?

1012. Are the necessary foundations in place to ensure the sustainability of the results of the programme?

1013. Propriety: who needs to be involved in the evaluation to be ethical?

1014. Have operating capacities been created and/or reinforced in partners?

1015. How were collaborations developed, and how are they sustained?

1016. Is the program in place as intended?

1017. Is there adequate validation on required fields?

1018. Does the solution fit in with organizations technical architectural requirements?

1019. Are there areas that need improvement?

1020. How is agile portfolio management done?

1021. What good practices or successful experiences or transferable examples have been identified?

1022. What is the expected monetary value of the Team Communication project?

1023. Mitigate. what will you do to minimize the impact should a risk event occur?

1024. What resources (both financial and non-financial) are available/needed?

1025. How should needs be met?

4.1 Project Performance Report: Team Communication

1026. To what degree do the goals specify concrete team work products?

1027. To what degree does the teams work approach provide opportunity for members to engage in open interaction?

1028. To what degree will the approach capitalize on and enhance the skills of all team members in a manner that takes into consideration other demands on members of the team?

1029. To what degree will the team ensure that all members equitably share the work essential to the success of the team?

1030. To what degree can team members meet frequently enough to accomplish the teams ends?

1031. What degree are the relative importance and priority of the goals clear to all team members?

1032. To what degree will each member have the opportunity to advance his or her professional skills in all three of the above categories while contributing to the accomplishment of the teams purpose and goals?

1033. To what degree do members articulate the goals beyond the team membership?

1034. What is the degree to which rules govern information exchange between groups?

1035. To what degree can team members frequently and easily communicate with one another?

1036. To what degree does the teams work approach provide opportunity for members to engage in results-based evaluation?

1037. To what degree is there a sense that only the team can succeed?

1038. To what degree are the goals ambitious?

4.2 Variance Analysis: Team Communication

1039. What are the actual costs to date?

1040. What is the performance to date and material commitment?

1041. What can be the cause of an increase in costs?

1042. Are the requirements for all items of overhead established by rational, traceable processes?

1043. What is your organizations rationale for sharing expenses and services between business segments?

1044. Are the actual costs used for variance analysis reconcilable with data from the accounting system?

1045. Are the bases and rates for allocating costs from each indirect pool consistently applied?

1046. Does the contractors system include procedures for measuring the performance of critical subcontractors?

1047. How do you manage changes in the nature of the overhead requirements?

1048. Why are standard cost systems used?

1049. Did an existing competitor change strategy?

1050. Can process improvements lead to unfavorable variances?

1051. How do you evaluate the impact of schedule changes, work around, et?

1052. Who are responsible for the establishment of budgets and assignment of resources for overhead performance?

1053. What does an unfavorable overhead volume variance mean?

1054. Are there quarterly budgets with quarterly performance comparisons?

1055. Is there a logical explanation for any variance?

1056. Are all cwbs elements specified for external reporting?

1057. Are estimates of costs at completion generated in a rational, consistent manner?

4.3 Earned Value Status: Team Communication

1058. Validation is a process of ensuring that the developed system will actually achieve the stakeholders desired outcomes; Are you building the right product? What do you validate?

1059. Where are your problem areas?

1060. Earned value can be used in almost any Team Communication project situation and in almost any Team Communication project environment. it may be used on large Team Communication projects, medium sized Team Communication projects, tiny Team Communication projects (in cut-down form), complex and simple Team Communication projects and in any market sector. some people, of course, know all about earned value, they have used it for years - but perhaps not as effectively as they could have?

1061. Where is evidence-based earned value in your organization reported?

1062. Are you hitting your Team Communication projects targets?

1063. What is the unit of forecast value?

1064. How much is it going to cost by the finish?

1065. If earned value management (EVM) is so good in determining the true status of a Team Communication project and Team Communication project its completion, why is it that hardly any one uses it in information systems related Team Communication projects?

1066. When is it going to finish?

1067. How does this compare with other Team Communication projects?

1068. Verification is a process of ensuring that the developed system satisfies the stakeholders agreements and specifications; Are you building the product right? What do you verify?

4.4 Risk Audit: Team Communication

1069. How risk averse are you?

1070. Do you have a consistent repeatable process that is actually used?

1071. Do you have an emergency plan?

1072. Do industry specialists and business risk auditors enhance audit reporting accuracy?

1073. What are the costs associated with late delivery or a defective product?

1074. Will participants be required to sign a legally counselled waiver or risk disclaimer when entering an event?

1075. Has risk management been considered when planning an event?

1076. How do you govern assets?

1077. Assessing risk with analytical procedures: do systemsthinking tools help auditors focus on diagnostic patterns?

1078. Do requirements demand the use of new analysis, design, or testing methods?

1079. What are the differences and similarities between strategic and operational risks in your organization?

1080. Are duties out-of-class?

1081. Have reasonable steps been taken to reduce the risks to acceptable levels?

1082. What events or circumstances could affect the achievement of your objectives?

1083. Are procedures in place to ensure the security of staff and information and compliance with privacy legislation if applicable?

1084. For paid staff, does your organization comply with the minimum conditions for employment and/or the applicable modern award?

1085. Estimated size of product in number of programs, files, transactions?

1086. Is the technology to be built new to your organization?

1087. Is the number of people on the Team Communication project team adequate to do the job?

4.5 Contractor Status Report: Team Communication

1088. What was the final actual cost?

1089. Are there contractual transfer concerns?

1090. What was the overall budget or estimated cost?

1091. Describe how often regular updates are made to the proposed solution. Are corresponding regular updates included in the standard maintenance plan?

1092. How does the proposed individual meet each requirement?

1093. What are the minimum and optimal bandwidth requirements for the proposed solution?

1094. How long have you been using the services?

1095. What was the actual budget or estimated cost for your organizations services?

1096. What process manages the contracts?

1097. If applicable; describe your standard schedule for new software version releases. Are new software version releases included in the standard maintenance plan?

1098. What is the average response time for answering a support call?

1099. How is risk transferred?

1100. Who can list a Team Communication project as organization experience, your organization or a previous employee of your organization?

1101. What was the budget or estimated cost for your organizations services?

4.6 Formal Acceptance: Team Communication

1102. Did the Team Communication project achieve its MOV?

1103. What function(s) does it fill or meet?

1104. Does it do what client said it would?

1105. What features, practices, and processes proved to be strengths or weaknesses?

1106. Who would use it?

1107. How does your team plan to obtain formal acceptance on your Team Communication project?

1108. What are the requirements against which to test, Who will execute?

1109. General estimate of the costs and times to complete the Team Communication project?

1110. How well did the team follow the methodology?

1111. Did the Team Communication project manager and team act in a professional and ethical manner?

1112. Who supplies data?

1113. Was the Team Communication project managed well?

1114. Do you perform formal acceptance or burn-in tests?

1115. Have all comments been addressed?

1116. What lessons were learned about your Team Communication project management methodology?

1117. Was the Team Communication project goal achieved?

1118. Do you buy-in installation services?

1119. Was the client satisfied with the Team Communication project results?

1120. Was the sponsor/customer satisfied?

1121. Is formal acceptance of the Team Communication project product documented and distributed?

5.0 Closing Process Group: Team Communication

1122. What areas does the group agree are the biggest success on the Team Communication project?

1123. Based on your Team Communication project communication management plan, what worked well?

1124. What were things that you need to improve?

1125. How critical is the Team Communication project success to the success of your organization?

1126. Is the Team Communication project funded?

1127. How well did the chosen processes fit the needs of the Team Communication project?

1128. What is the Team Communication project name and date of completion?

1129. What level of risk does the proposed budget represent to the Team Communication project?

1130. When will the Team Communication project be done?

1131. Just how important is your work to the overall success of the Team Communication project?

1132. Is there a clear cause and effect between the

activity and the lesson learned?

1133. What will you do to minimize the impact should a risk event occur?

1134. What is the risk of failure to your organization?

1135. Are there funding or time constraints?

1136. Is this a follow-on to a previous Team Communication project?

1137. What will you do?

1138. Did the delivered product meet the specified requirements and goals of the Team Communication project?

5.1 Procurement Audit: Team Communication

1139. Where applicable, did your organization adequately manage experts employed to assist in the procurement process?

1140. Did your organization state the minimum requirements to be met by the variants in the tender documents?

1141. Were the performance conditions under the contract comprehensive and unambiguous?

1142. Does procurement staff have skills to procure complex or special items (i.e. IT)?

1143. Is the procurement process well organized?

1144. Are all purchase orders accounted for?

1145. Are staff members evaluated in accordance with the terms of existing negotiated agreements?

1146. Were products/services not received within the prescribed time limit?

1147. Is it calculated whether aggregated procurement can be more cost-efficient?

1148. Are there reasonable procedures to identify possible sources of supply?

1149. Is the departments procurement function/unit well organized?

1150. Does the procurement function/unit have the ability to apply electronic procurement?

1151. Is the routing of copies of purchase order forms defined?

1152. Is the accounting distribution of expenses included with the request for payment?

1153. Is the purchasing department organizationally independent of the departments using that function?

1154. Are there systems for recording and monitoring in order to discover malpractice and fraud in the procurement function/unit?

1155. Has an upper limit of cost been fixed?

1156. Is a cost/benefit analysis, a cost/effectiveness or a financial analysis considering life-cycle costs performed and is the funding of the procurement guaranteed?

1157. Is there no evidence of any individual on the evaluation panel being biased?

1158. Does your organization have an administrative timetable to assist the staff in implementing the budget calendar?

5.2 Contract Close-Out: Team Communication

1159. What happens to the recipient of services?

1160. Was the contract type appropriate?

1161. Change in circumstances?

1162. Have all contract records been included in the Team Communication project archives?

1163. Have all contracts been closed?

1164. Parties: Authorized?

1165. How does it work?

1166. How is the contracting office notified of the automatic contract close-out?

1167. Have all acceptance criteria been met prior to final payment to contractors?

1168. Was the contract complete without requiring numerous changes and revisions?

1169. Change in attitude or behavior?

1170. Why Outsource?

1171. Has each contract been audited to verify acceptance and delivery?

1172. Are the signers the authorized officials?

1173. Was the contract sufficiently clear so as not to result in numerous disputes and misunderstandings?

1174. What is capture management?

1175. How/when used ?

1176. Change in knowledge?

1177. Parties: who is involved?

1178. Have all contracts been completed?

5.3 Project or Phase Close-Out: Team Communication

1179. Who controlled key decisions that were made?

1180. Were messages directly related to the release strategy or phases of the Team Communication project?

1181. Does the lesson educate others to improve performance?

1182. If you were the Team Communication project sponsor, how would you determine which Team Communication project team(s) and/or individuals deserve recognition?

1183. Can the lesson learned be replicated?

1184. Were cost budgets met?

1185. What is a Risk Management Process?

1186. What security considerations needed to be addressed during the procurement life cycle?

1187. What advantages do the an individual interview have over a group meeting, and vice-versa?

1188. What stakeholder group needs, expectations, and interests are being met by the Team Communication project?

1189. What were the desired outcomes?

1190. Who are the Team Communication project stakeholders and what are roles and involvement?

1191. What could be done to improve the process?

1192. Is the lesson significant, valid, and applicable?

1193. What process was planned for managing issues/risks?

1194. Does the lesson describe a function that would be done differently the next time?

1195. Was the schedule met?

1196. What could have been improved?

1197. Who is responsible for award close-out?

5.4 Lessons Learned: Team Communication

1198. Was any formal risk assessment carried out at the start of the Team Communication project, and was this followed up during the Team Communication project?

1199. Recommendation: what do you recommend should be done to ensure that others throughout your organization can benefit from what you have learned?

1200. Were the Team Communication project objectives met (if not, briefly account for what wasnt met)?

1201. How effective were the communications materials in providing and orienting team members about the details of the Team Communication project?

1202. How does the budget cycle affect the case?

1203. How was the quality of products/processes assured?

1204. How complete and timely were the materials you were provided to decide whether to proceed from one Team Communication project lifecycle phase to the next?

1205. How useful and complete was the Team

Communication project document repository?

1206. For the next Team Communication project, how could you improve on the way Team Communication project was conducted?

1207. How effective was the acceptance management process?

1208. If you had to do this Team Communication project again, what is the one thing that you would change (related to process, not to technical solutions)?

1209. How well does the product or service the Team Communication project produced meet your needs?

1210. How effectively were issues managed on the Team Communication project?

1211. How often do communications get lost?

1212. Where could you improve?

1213. Overall, how effective were the efforts to prepare you and your organization for the impact of the product/service of the Team Communication project?

1214. How many interest groups are stakeholders?

1215. Are you in full regulatory compliance?

1216. Was there enough support – guidance, clerical support, training?

Index

improved   79, 84-85, 89, 102, 226, 258
improving   79, 169, 217
incentives   98
include   16, 84, 87, 135, 137, 155-156, 209-210, 241
included   2, 7, 52, 142, 147, 171, 179, 197, 215, 219, 247, 254-255
INCLUDES   9
including   18, 30, 32, 36, 43, 52, 61, 95, 98, 148, 155, 201, 212
increase   84, 121, 147, 241
increased   111, 192
increasing   107, 224
incurred   45
Incurrence   189
in-depth   8, 10
indicate   63, 93, 109
indicated   94
indicators   20, 42, 54, 63-64, 70, 82, 98, 151
indirect   52, 152, 189, 241
indirectly   1
individual   1, 54, 157, 183, 194, 207, 231, 247, 254, 257
industry   94, 112, 160, 175, 245
infinite 113
influence   78, 111, 130, 137, 196, 224, 235
influences   161, 230
inform 233
informed   122, 126
ingrained   98
inherent   191
initial   38, 118
initially 38
initiated   179, 222
Initiating   2, 114, 126
initiative   10, 128, 183, 187-188, 235
Innovate   74
innovation   49, 61-62, 89, 98, 183
innovative   115, 171, 179, 215
in-process   70
inputs   37, 39, 53, 69, 94
insight 60, 67
insights 8
inspection   137
Instead112

281

management 1, 3-5, 8-9, 22-23, 30, 36, 47, 60, 62, 64-65, 70-71, 76-77, 79-80, 84, 86, 88-89, 106, 118-119, 133-139, 145-146, 148, 154-155, 166, 168, 170, 173, 175-176, 178, 182-183, 190, 192-195, 197, 204, 207-208, 211, 213, 215, 218, 223, 225-226, 233, 238, 243, 245, 250-251, 256-257, 260
manager   7, 9, 16, 33-34, 122, 140, 145, 169, 218, 249
managers   2, 125, 176, 198, 202, 207, 216
manages   82, 88, 135, 247
managing   2, 81, 125, 130, 140, 211, 258
mandatory   222
manner   17, 80, 189, 193, 219, 225, 239, 242, 249
mantle 117
manuals   226
mapping   58, 69
market 20, 132, 160, 232, 243
marketer   7
Marketing   111, 160
markets   131
Maslow   169
material   189, 210, 241
materials   1, 146, 230, 259
matrices   143
Matrix 2-5, 131, 143, 189, 203
matter 40, 42, 54
matters   223
maximize   202, 233
maximizing   113
McClellan   169
McGregor   169
meaning   159
meaningful   46, 123, 151
measurable   29, 39, 126, 129, 226, 232
measure   2, 9, 17, 23, 35, 39, 42, 44-45, 48-49, 51, 53-54, 61-62, 74, 78, 85-86, 91, 95, 102, 179-181, 184-186
measured   16, 43, 47-48, 50, 53, 55, 79, 94, 102, 151
measures   42-43, 45-46, 51, 54, 61, 63-64, 70, 72, 82, 93, 98, 155, 185, 188, 199, 205, 215-216, 234
measuring   94, 151, 241
mechanical   1
mechanics   220
mechanized   175
medical   225
medium   243

months79, 86
Morale 131
motivate   111
motivation   21, 93
motive 187
moving   110
multiple   183, 225, 233
mutual 133
narrow 60
national   131, 215
nature 241
nearest   11
nearly 123
necessary   59-60, 70, 81, 115, 120, 122, 137, 180, 182, 198,
201, 211, 237
needed   17, 19, 21-22, 24-25, 37, 62, 67, 69, 93, 97, 100,
142, 169, 172, 177, 196, 207-208, 238, 257
negative   174, 213
negatively   200
negotiated   109, 214, 253
neither 1
network   3, 162-163
Neutral10, 15, 26, 42, 57, 74, 91, 104
nonlinear   185
normal 98
notice 1, 134
noticing   224
notified   255
number   25, 41, 43, 55, 72, 89, 103, 123, 197, 230, 246, 262
numbers   104, 230
numerous   255-256
objection   20, 23
objective   7, 44, 190, 197, 204, 224, 237
objectives   16, 20, 22, 26, 36, 39, 60, 72, 95, 99, 109, 115, 119,
131, 134, 137, 147, 181, 200, 205, 218, 227, 229, 232, 246, 259
observed   85
observing   212
obsolete   106
obstacles   17, 171, 179
obtain 118, 249
obtained   34, 211
obtaining   52
obviously   10

qualifies   62, 67
qualify 52, 65, 68
qualities   234
quality 1, 4-5, 9, 17, 45-46, 55, 65-67, 70, 79, 93, 97, 107, 127, 137-
138, 154, 174-175, 183, 185, 187, 193, 201, 207, 215, 223, 225, 259
quantified   100
quantify   52
quantity   210
quarterly   242
question   10, 15, 26, 42, 57, 74, 91, 104, 109, 132, 187
questions   7-8, 10, 72, 209
quickly 9, 58, 66, 71, 177, 198
radically   64
rather 122
rational   241-242
rationale   208, 223, 241
reached   22
reaching   214
reactivate   112
readiness   36, 137
readings   92, 134
realistic   22, 62, 104, 174, 202
Reality 231
realize 53
really   7, 19, 35
reason 109
reasonable   75, 148, 175, 246, 253
reasons   36, 193
re-assign   158
rebuild 115
recasts 177
receive   8-9, 34, 44, 196, 213
received   27, 169, 198, 231, 253
recipient   19, 255
recognised   80
recognize   2, 15-16, 20, 23, 84
recognized   17-19, 23-25, 67, 175, 232, 236
recognizes   16
recommend   122, 259
record 183, 187
recorded   184, 220
recording   1, 254
records   69, 123, 151, 190, 225, 255

repository   260
represent   79, 182, 221, 251
reproduced   1
reputation   119
request   5, 72, 140, 181-182, 219-222, 254
requested   1, 84, 219, 221
requests   219-220
require 28, 52, 59, 70, 92, 97, 164, 214
required   23, 26, 31-32, 36, 50, 66, 68, 84, 89, 93, 126, 132,
142, 157-158, 172-173, 186-187, 193, 197, 237, 245
requires   127, 210
requiring   130, 255
research   20, 115, 121, 132, 225
Reserve   177
reserved   1
reserves   190
reside 86
resilient213
resolution   60, 80
resolve 22, 25, 158, 228-229
resolved   173, 198
Resource   3-4, 112, 155, 158, 164, 166-167, 193, 217
resourced   225
resources   2, 7, 18, 20-21, 28, 40-41, 54, 62, 89, 93, 96, 99,
105, 110, 112-113, 127, 132, 140, 142, 157, 159, 169, 172, 180,
208, 228, 238, 242
respect   1
respective   133
respond   134, 213
responded   11
responding   200
response   16, 20, 92-94, 99, 213, 247
responses   86, 199
responsive   179
result /1, /9, 179, 195, 221, 226, 256
resulted   100
resulting   70, 133
results 8, 29-30, 64, 74, 77, 79, 82-84, 87-89, 96, 98, 133, 177-178,
180, 184, 187, 190, 215, 226, 237, 250
Retain 104
retained   63
retention   46
retrospect   123

CPSIA information can be obtained
at www.ICGtesting.com
Printed in the USA
BVHW091740270819
556849BV00006B/210/P